PORCELAIN

Jack Doherty

A & C Black · London

University of Pennsylvania Press · Philadelphia

First published in Great Britain 2002
A & C Black Publishers Limited
37 Soho Square
London W1D 3QZ
www.acblack.com

ISBN 0-7136-5085-0

Published simultaneously in the USA by
University of Pennsylvania Press
4200 Pine Street
Philadelphia, PA 19104-4011

ISBN 0-8122-1827-2

Cover illustration: Porcelain jug by Jack
  Doherty. *Photograph by Sue Packer.*

Back illustration: Caroline Whyman. Ovaled
  forms with gold, platinum and bronze
  lustre.

Frontispiece: Jack Doherty. Soda-fired porcelain cup. Height: 15 cm (6 in.).

Design by Alan Hamp
Cover design by Dorothy Moir

Printed and bound in Singapore by
Tien Wan Press Ltd

738.2DOH

PORCELAIN

Sasha Wardell

Soda Glazing
Ruthanne Tudball

Throwing Pots
Phil Rogers

Contents

Acknowledgments

I want to say thank you to all the ceramicists who have so generously provided photographs and information for this book. Also to Alan Ault of Valentines Clay and Harry Fraser of Potclays Ltd for their technical support. I am grateful to Helen Brown of the Cheltenham Art Gallery and Museum for pictures and information on historical pieces and to Galerie Besson for providing images of some contemporary work.

I would also like to apologise to all the people who I bored with the project, especially Ellen who tried hard to organise me, Jake who made sure there was always a glass of wine and Joan, the most literate potter that I know.

Introduction

Porcelain is, by reputation, the most difficult and capricious of ceramic materials. The technical literature of studio ceramics abounds with such warnings, but the high quality of some modern commercially produced porcelain clay bodies has debunked many of the long held myths about its workability. In recent years the availability of these clay bodies has made porcelain more accessible to studio ceramicists, and their improving quality has helped to make production by hand easier, but it still holds many mysteries. Certainly porcelain makes demands on the sensitivity and skill of the maker, and requires attention and care at every stage of production. Perhaps more than any other clay it alters and changes during all stages of making. It has a greater shrinkage than stoneware or earthenware, a propensity to warp and distort in the kiln, but it does undergo an almost magical transformation during the firing. It becomes a substance that has as much in common with glass as it does with clay.

When I began to think about the content of this book I had to make decisions about what to include, and I decided that this was not the place to consider in detail the work of the great porcelain factories. Where industrial methods are illustrated, they have not been included to demonstrate production techniques, but rather to show the aesthetic qualities of a particular designer's or artist's work. The work that will feature in this book is essentially studio produced porcelain, individually designed and made, using the widest range of handmaking processes. On asking the question, 'what is porcelain?', I quickly found ten differing definitions. I also asked a number of eminent porcelain makers to describe the particular qualities of the material that excited them and inspired their work. Their answers highlighted a number of key words: purity, fineness, translucency, whiteness, strength, hardness and durability when fired. These were the physical properties most often described, the classic attributes of high-fired porcelain. However in recent years it has become clear that many inventive ceramicists are challenging the preconceptions surrounding our definitions of porcelain and are selecting and using new forming and firing methods which exploit other qualities of the clay. Clarity of colour, softness when fired at low temperature, responsiveness to the subtlety of smoke and raku firing, have all become part of the language of contemporary porcelain makers.

It was important for me to look at the history and evolution of porcelain making, through my eyes as a potter, in turn delighted and repelled by some of the objects produced. I hope that historians will be lenient with my subjective and brief account.

To everyone who has provided

information and support, I would like to say thank you. I hope that by asking the right questions and relying on the experience and generosity of many fine makers, the information in this book will inform and inspire potters and ceramicists to explore and enjoy the special qualities of this sensuous and beautiful material.

Chapter One
History of Porcelain Making

China

The Chinese discovered porcelain, not dramatically, nor as the result of a fortunate accident; the knowledge needed to make porcelain accumulated slowly over several thousand years.

In Shang Dynasty China (17th –11th centuries BC), potters were producing a white unglazed ceramic. While the period is noted for the production of bronze, there were developments in ceramic technology, particularly in kiln design—perhaps as a spin off from the metal industries—which were significant in the much later development of porcelain. Shang wares were found at Anyang in the Henan province; ritual rather than domestic pieces, they were handbuilt with a carved decoration and were similar in both form and decoration to ritual bronzes. They were made from a clay body containing kaolin and were probably fired no higher than 1200°C/2192°F. In his book *Chinese Glazes*, Nigel Wood compares the analysis of these clays with some porcelains of the Tang dynasty (AD618 –906) and suggests that they were similar in composition to some of their lower quality wares. He speculates that had kiln technology been more advanced and higher firing temperatures attainable, then the Shang wares could have been fully vitrified and translucent. Although it is from gradual improvements to white earthenware and light coloured stoneware clays that

porcelain evolved, there is little evidence of a developing white ware technology until the Tang dynasty some 1800 years later. A traveller writing in AD851 describes seeing 'vessels of clay as transparent as glass'. Three of the most important kiln sites of the northern Tang dynasty were at Gongxian in Henan province, Xing in Hebei province and Ding near to the town of Jiancicun. Gongxian is perhaps the world's earliest porcelain site, its wares dated to AD575. Xing ware has become accepted as the purest of the northern Chinese porcelains. The site at Lingchen produced large quantities of work, making porcelain available to 'rich and poor alike'. There is evidence pointing to an increasing control of quality, the selection and refinement of materials, and the use of slips to improve whiteness. The control of kiln atmosphere and the use of reduction firing became a factor contributing to the characteristic cooler tone of the Xing porcelains.

It is certain that refined and translucent porcelains were produced during the Tang dynasty, but it was not until the Song dynasty (960–1279) that porcelain makers achieved the mastery of materials and technique which prompted Bernard Leach to write, 'Of all pottery, that of the Song period is most expressive of its material, it is in fact the purest of pottery.' This was one of the great periods in Chinese ceramic history. In later centuries while potters developed a wider range of technique, greater control and refinement, the freshness and clarity of form and purity of glaze and colour leave Song porcelains unsurpassed.

In Northern China the Ding kilns which began production in the early 8th century, and made whiteware influenced by the Xing tradition, developed one of the most refined and beautiful porcelains. Production techniques evolved which included inventive combinations of throwing and moulding. Thrown forms were beaten onto carved and incised moulds transferring complex and delicate decorations. Kiln packing and firing procedures were also revolutionised by later Ding potters, who introduced sophisticated saggars able to contain several pieces of descending size, thus increasing the kiln output. They pioneered the technique of stacking ware on its rim, so reducing the risk of warping. The disadvantage of this way of firing, however, was that the unglazed rim, wiped clear of glaze to prevent sticking to the saggar, left a rough edge. Sheet copper or occasionally gold or silver was cut and fitted to the rims, enhancing the status of these vessels. As well as white and cream ware, Ding potters also produced exquisite coloured porcelains—'purple Ding' with a russet or persimmon surface, and the extremely rare black iron glazed porcelain, even in its own time described as being 'rare as a black swan'.

Jingdezhen in the north east of Jiangxi province was one of the earliest production centres for porcelain in Southern China. Superbly situated, close to sources of kaolin, petunse and ample supplies of wood for kiln fuel, it was destined to become the pottery and porcelain making capital of the world.

The materials used were significantly different from those used in the north. The early works were made from porcelain stones which were quartz/mica mixtures containing little of the clay minerals that constituted a large part of the raw material of northern porcelain. The word petunse or 'little white bricks' is often used to describe these stones which were used with no additions of clay, just prepared for use by crushing and levigating. Among the most famous Jingdezhen wares are the yingqing pieces with their carved or applied decorations and 'shadow blue' glazes, which were produced from the 10th–14th centuries AD. This colour developed in reduction firing from the iron bearing minerals used to make the glazes.

The Yuan dynasty (AD1280–1367) saw many changes and innovations in the decorative arts in China. The centre of pottery activity moved to the south, the industry at Jingdezhen expanding rapidly. A new porcelain called shu-fu evolved, with moulded or incised decoration under a thick glaze. The period also saw the rise in popularity of underglaze cobalt blue decoration. The earliest use of cobalt as a painting pigment (which was probably imported from the Middle East) was found in fragments dating to the late 8th or early 9th century AD. In the Yuan dynasty it was applied to fine white porcelains of the shu-fu type. This ware quickly became the most popular of all Chinese ceramics, acclaimed both at home and abroad and exported to the Middle East and to South East Asia.

The Ming Dynasty (AD1369–1644) lasted for almost 300 years and was a period of expansion, prosperity and creative activity in China. Secure trade routes and increased contact with the

outside world led to a massive increase in the production and export of porcelain. The huge demand from both domestic and export markets made Jingdezhen the source of the world's porcelain. In a letter written in 1712, the Jesuit priest Père d'Entrecolles wrote, 'the whirling flames and smoke which rise at different places make the approach to Jingdezhen remarkable for its extent, depth, and shape. During a night entrance, one thinks that the

Chinese, 14th-century charger with blue and white decoration, 1325-55. Made for export to India. *Photograph courtesy of Cheltenham Art Gallery & Museum, Gloucestershire, UK/Bridgeman Art Library.*

whole city is on fire, or that it is one large furnace with many vent holes.' While both blue and white, and red and white ceramics had been made earlier, the style reached its peak during the Ming Dynasty. The innovation of

Chinese, 19th-century covered jar with a famille rose enamelled decoration, 1800-50.
Photograph courtesy of Cheltenham Art Gallery & Museum, UK/Bridgeman Art Library.

Jingdezhen potters was not in tech–nique, but in the way that these processes were used to create calligraphic, floral and abstract designs. The use of overglaze enamels was developed and perfected during the latter part of the 15th century.

Korea

Korea was the second country to produce porcelain. Chinese ceramics were being imported into Korea from the 3rd and 4th centuries AD and were used as models by Korean potters. The high regard for porcelain in Korea dates to the Koryo period AD918–1392, when Korean potters had limited success in producing their own quality porcelain. Large quantities of Chinese wares were imported to meet a growing demand. Korean potters used these porcelains as models, as they had done in the past, accepting Chinese ceramic culture and technology in order to further their own progress. By the end of the 12th century, typically Korean porcelains were being made, and by the 15th century under the reign of King Sejong of Choson, a truly distinctive white porcelain was being produced. The best Korean work was directed towards revealing the essence of the clay, glaze and pigment. Although in demand by the public, its general use was prohibited by court order for a time. A census of potteries carried out in AD1424 listed 324 kilns across the country, of which 139 produced porcelain.

The Japanese invasion of Korea in 1592 effectively destroyed the porcelain industry. Some 400 potters were taken to Japan as prisoners, a great impetus to the industry there. A further invasion from China in 1636 compounded an already dire situation; the ceramics industry had to wait to be rebuilt from the ruins of two major wars. When porcelain production resumed, changes were apparent in the work. The forms had a vigour and vitality, and the pure white or blue and white glaze had a fresh warmth and depth. The range of ware produced included large jars, and stationery objects such as water droppers and brush stands. At this time porcelain began to be used by commoners in ancestral rites.

In the middle of the 18th century the official state factory was moved to a site on the Han river. By 1883 it had become too expensive to be subsidised by state funds and a private management system was introduced. The end of state funding and the use of new processes such as printed transfer decoration led to the loss of traditional skills and the decline of the industry.

Japan

Porcelain making started in Japan in the early 17th century. Legend has it that a Korean potter, Li Sappei, discovered porcelain stone in the Arita area of Northern Kyushu. It is probable, however, that porcelain made from materials imported from Southern China had been fired earlier in the 16th century. The skills of making, firing and decoration using both underglaze cobalt painting and onglaze enamels were provided by Chinese and Korean craftsmen. Before the introduction of porcelain, both of these forms of decoration were unknown in Japan. Political turmoil in China in the middle of the 17th century, as the Ming Dynasty collapsed, forced European traders to seek new sources of Oriental porcelain, and in a few decades porcelain making flourished in Japan.

This new industry was patronised and protected by the feudal lords of Kyushu. Punishment for stealing production secrets from a feudal domain were severe, but a few porcelain workshops did start in other parts of Japan. The wares made at Arita are known in the West as Imari, after the port from which they were shipped. Although the skills of forming and decorating were taught by Chinese and Korean potters, a true Japanese style quickly emerged. Sakaida Kakiemon developed a way of decorating with overglaze enamels. Typical colours include iron red, soft blue and yellow, with a little gilding. The style was continued by his family and since many of them were also called Kakiemon it has become known by that name. Famous early Kakiemon decorations include patterns using sprigs of foliage and quails, which influenced the decorative style of several European factories including Worcester in England, Meissen in Germany and Chantilly in France.

Europe

Porcelain was brought to Europe from China throughout most of the 17th century, shipped as ballast in the holds of East India Company vessels, which were carrying cargoes of silk and tea. It was brought in increasing quantities, which fuelled the passion but never satisfied the demand for this 'white gold'. From our perspective it is difficult to fully appreciate the sense of wonder and excitement felt for this precious material. It was the material of a luxury art form. To own a porcelain collection was a signal of privilege, to own a porcelain factory was the desire of kings.

Given the high prestige and the commercial value attached to Chinese porcelain, it was inevitable that, in Europe, serious attempts would be made to discover the secrets of its manufacture. The earliest attempts to develop a workable clay body involved using materials such as alabaster and glass based frits, which were added to light burning materials, then fired at low temperatures. These soft porcelains had a limited firing range, distorting or collapsing if overfired. Some were also likely to crack in contact with hot water. While not even close to their oriental models in composition, some soft paste porcelains were beautiful materials in their own right. Heavy kiln losses and high production costs meant that few factories survived for any length of time.

The earliest successful attempts to make a form of porcelain in Europe occurred in Italy. Under the patronage of Francesco I de Medici, a soft paste porcelain was made in Florence in the late 16th century. It is thought that the clay used contained powdered glass, rock crystal and sand, with clay from Vicenza, and a white earth from Faenza. Production was limited. The few surviving examples include jugs, bowls, plates and decorative plaques. Medici porcelain is usually blue and white, reflecting influences from Persia, China and indigenous maiolica.

In Rouen, France, c. 1673, Louis Porerat continued the tradition of soft paste European porcelain. Further early factories were established at Saint Cloud, Villeroy Ménnecy and Vicennes Sèvres. These factories had substantial patronage, often producing wares for court use.

In Britain, a soft paste using bone ash, Cornish stone and China clay was perfected. Since the middle of the 18th century, soft paste porcelain has been made, first in London at Bow, Chelsea and Limehouse. Other factories developed at Newcastle-under-Lyme, Longton Hall, Derby, and Liverpool. The factory established by Dr John Wall and William Davis at Worcester in 1751 used a clay body with steatite as a flux. This gave a more robust material, which could be finely potted. An impressive range of functional pieces, tablewares, sauceboats and pickle dishes was produced. Many were decorated with variations of the popular 'willow pattern'. In the latter part of the 19th century the factory developed its famous 'Japan' designs using adaptations of Kakiemon and Imari patterns and colouring. A high temperature porcelain was developed to make functional tablewares and laboratory equipment.

The technical refinement of bone china is attributed to Josiah Spode 1755–1827. The Spode factory at Stoke-on-Trent was established in 1761 to produce earthenware. Under Josiah Spode's direction it began making decorative and functional bone china wares at the beginning of the 19th century, as it continues to do today.

The rage for porcelain and the mysteries surrounding its making spawned the wildest tales, for example that a porcelain cup was incapable of holding poison. It is fitting in a way that its European inventor was an alchemist whose search for the philosopher's stone led by a torturous and self-destructive route to the discovery of the secrets of true porcelain.

Johann Friedrich Böttger (1682–1719) was a chemist and a self-proclaimed alchemist who was employed, and at times imprisoned, by Augustus the Strong, Elector of Saxony and King of Poland and charged with the task of making gold. His failure to achieve this led to threats on his life.

Böttger made the claim that he could make porcelain. The status of porcelain was probably second only to gold and Augustus agreed to sponsor his research. Böttger collaborated with the scientist Ehenfried Walter von Tschirnhausen (1651–1705).

They understood the principle that Oriental porcelain was made by vitrifying natural minerals at high temperature, and began a systematic series of tests and a search for suitable raw materials. They also knew that kiln technology was an important factor. A furnace had to be designed, built and fired which would be capable of reaching the necessary firing temperatures. In the future, wherever a porcelain factory succeeded, it was not just with the information required to make a workable clay, but also relied on the presence of a kiln master who was capable of organizing the firing of the ware. Working in extraordinarily bad conditions, Böttger and Tschirnhausen produced a high temperature red stoneware which they called red porcelain. Böttger's stoneware was a beautiful material in its own right, cold to the touch and hard enough to be cut and polished like a precious stone. The last remaining part of the puzzle was solved when they discovered a white burning clay from Colditz. Under the patronage of Augustus the Strong, the Meissen porcelain factory was established in 1710 with Johann Böttger as its technical director. For 40 years, Saxon porcelain (or Dresden china as it is called in Britain) remained without serious competition. Much of the subsequent development work was carried out by Johann Gregorius Horoldt (1696–1775), a painter and colour chemist who worked to improve the enamelling process and to enlarge the range of available colours. The zenith of production was, perhaps, during the 1730s when Johann Joachim Kändler was the chief sculptor and modeller. He was an exceptionally talented artist whose vigorously modelled figures, often based on commedia dell'arte characters, set the standard for all the other factories.

USA

It is probable that early attempts to produce porcelain occurred in the USA in the first half of the 18th century. Andrew Duche, who was an earthenware potter from Georgia, is credited with discovering the method of porcelain making using local china clay. For a few years from 1770, soft paste porcelain was made by Bonnin and Morris in Philadelphia. While raw materials were available in the USA, the pioneer porcelain potters found great difficulties making and selling their ware. Skilled labour was scarce so some early workshops had to employ immigrant potters from Europe. As production became established, the fledgling industry faced intense competition from cheaper wares imported from England. Towards the end of the 19th century an industry was established with centres such as the Tucker and Hemphill works in Philadelphia, Cartlidge & Co. in New York, and the Union Porcelain works in Brooklyn. By the beginning of the 20th century, bone china was being produced in the United States comparable in quality to that which could be imported from Europe.

Chapter Two
Development of Studio Porcelain

From our standpoint in time, it is difficult to imagine the effect of porcelain when it was first imported in quantity from China during the 17th century. It ranked with silver in the esteem of the rich and sparked a cult which inspired changes in style and fashion.

Throughout Europe the discovery of porcelain led to the establishment of important production centres. The great factories produced work to satisfy the demand for high quality objects, fuelled by what seemed an inexhaustible interest in artefacts made from porcelain. A European industry evolved that, while it has always included the creative artist and craftsman, developed more sophisticated production techniques and materials to suit the needs of industry. Clays were designed for slipcasting, and glazing and decorating techniques reflected a desire for increasing refinement.

Bernard Leach. Fluted bowl with white glaze, Diameter: 15 cm (6 in.).

Some of the most influential steps in establishing a studio pottery tradition were made by Bernard Leach (1887–1979) at his St Ives pottery in the UK. Leach, with his passion for the forms and glazes of the Song Dynasty in China, made porcelain pieces, bowls and bottles, with lively forms and austere surfaces radically different from highly designed factory made products. He worked with the clay in a direct and honest way, using the wheel and simple decorating techniques. His early pots, in a sense, validated porcelain as a medium for studio potters. At that time the technology of porcelain making was geared towards producing materials for industrial production. Leach had to find suitable raw materials and then design clays which were plastic enough to be thrown on the wheel. It is interesting that his research into materials using kaolins from Cornwall and ball clays from Dorset, and experiments with recipes, led to the production of clays which were similar in appearance to some of the earliest Chinese porcelains. The first St Ives porcelains were essentially proto-porcelains or porcellaneous stonewares which were not particularly translucent.

While Leach was a great pioneer of studio pottery and an early studio porcelain maker, the potter who made the most significant contribution to the development of wheel-thrown porcelain was Lucie Rie (1902–1995). Her Viennese upbringing and her modernist design education at the Kunstgewerbeschule inspired work which has a unique unity of form and surface decoration. She came to England in 1939 and established her studio in London. She mixed her own porcelain clays, based on Leach recipes. These were mixed in relatively small quantities by hand, using either potash or soda feldspar as a flux, each giving a different character to the fired glaze. Her experimental work with glazes produced rich and colourful surfaces – deep turquoises and sharp uranium yellows were typical. She was one of the first studio potters to successfully fire to high temperatures in an electric kiln. This, and her urban lifestyle, offered aspiring potters an alternative to the rural reduction firing idyll of the Leach followers.

David Leach (b.1911), Bernard's son, who was for many years responsible for running the Leach pottery, established his own workshop at Bovey Tracey in Devon. He uses porcelain to make refined and sophisticated domestic pots. His fluted and celadon-glazed tea sets show an individual approach which was in contrast to the popular rustic stoneware or earthenware of the period.

Excellent functional porcelain was made by Harry and May Davis, whose workshop was geared to producing thrown domestic ware competing in technical quality and price with industrial tableware. Geoffrey Whiting (1919– 88) also made porcelain tableware. His teapots, in particular, with their refined forms and subtle painted decoration are still regarded as exemplary. Gwyn Hanssen made porcelain tablewares in her early workshops in England and France. Her work then was influenced by the wood-fired, lightly salt-glazed domestic wares from La Borne in central France.

There were few readymade clays available to porcelain makers until the 1970s. Potters' merchants and suppliers dealt more with industry, and their business with studio potters supported stoneware or earthenware production. Potters who had an interest in porcelain, generally as a subsidiary product to a stoneware range, made their own clay body and there was great debate about a definition for porcelain. It seemed important at that time to describe the properties which make porcelain different from other clays. An early issue of Ceramic Review featured ten different statements defining porcelain of which perhaps the most durable came from Bernard Leach, writing in *A Potter's Book*, 'The word porcelain applies to pottery which is white, vitrified and translucent.' The introduction of the industrially produced 'David Leach' porcelain clay offered a new material and fresh creative possibilities to potters and students. There were very few potters at this time interested in making useful porcelain wares. The material was seen as special, precious and expensive, to be used with care in the making of decorative pieces. This new clay demanded a fresh vision and appropriate ways of working. New techniques were added to the repertoire of studio potters. Modifying, press moulding and slipcasting were used to produce appropriate forms. Turning became a respectable process. Piercing, carving, scraping and even sand-papering extended the range of techniques which were being used.

Mary Rogers used deceptively simple handmaking techniques such as pinching and coiling to make refined decorative pieces. Her work was based on ideas derived from natural forms. She often made delicate bowl forms and developed a way of using painted oxides on the surface of her forms, adding to their organic quality. Other potters making work inspired by natural forms were Peter Simpson, Geoffrey Swindell and Deidre Burnett. Audrey Blackman specialised in making figures and figure groups using a rolled clay technique. The demands of this way of working led to the development of her own clay body which has high plasticity and whiteness.

Lucie Rie. Bowl with bronze rim, 1976.

Notable porcelain makers in Britain include Colin Pearson, whose thrown and altered work was among the first to use the material in a direct and spontaneous way. His forms, with their added wings, articulate the delicacy and fragility of the clay. A master of ceramic technology, he developed a range of glaze surfaces for lower temperature firings in an electric kiln, producing beautiful blues and turquoises using lithium carbonate.

Peter Lane is a potter and author who has done much to promote the appreciation and understanding of contemporary porcelain. His refined thrown and turned bowl forms, often with airbrushed surfaces, are the product of his meticulous approach, careful control of the quality of the material, and precise and accurate way of working.

In the USA, Rudy Staffel is an influential figure. His 'light gatherers' are among today's most inventive porcelain works. They exploit the translucency of the fired clay, catching the light within vessel forms which are thrown and built from thick and thin strips and patches of clay. Ruth Duckworth began her career in Britain and made sculpture from clay in the 1950s, but the greater part of her working life has been spent in the USA. Trained as a sculptor, she uses porcelain in many of her smaller, subtle abstract forms. Byron Temple was an apprentice at the Leach pottery in St Ives, England, before establishing his pottery in New Jersey. His thrown and altered lidded jar forms often have coloured cords sealing them, adding a mysterious and ritual quality.

On the continent of Europe the tradition of studio porcelain making is long established, an interesting feature of its development there being the creative and technical impetus derived from the collaboration between artist potters and industry. In Scandinavia, major ceramics manufacturing companies such as Arabia in Finland, Gustavberg in Sweden, and Bing and Grondahl in Denmark, created workspace for potters, artists and designers who were encouraged to

David Leach. Celadon-glazed porcelain bottle.

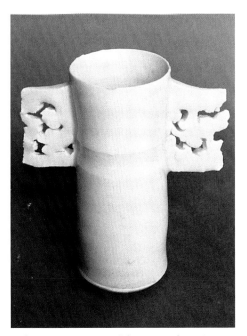

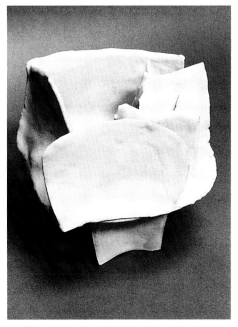

Colin Pearson. Winged form. Height: 14 cm (5 ½ in.).

Ruth Duckworth. Slab built form. Height: 19 cm (7 ½ in.).

develop forms and glazes with the support of the factories' chemists and technicians. Friedl Kjellberg, Lisbeth Munch Petersen and Auune Siimes are among those potters who each developed a particularly individual way of using porcelain.

In Germany there is a long-standing interest in porcelain making among artist potters, the influence of the Bauhaus having had a profound effect on them. Early studio porcelain makers whose work reflects ideas of uncluttered form and controlled glaze surfaces are Karl and Ursula Scheid. Their work follows the continental tradition of firing to temperatures well in excess of 1300°C/2372°F. The German industrial porcelain company Rosenthal has, for many years, encouraged co-operation between artists and industry. Beate Kuhn worked as a designer at Rosenthal before establishing her

own studio. Her porcelain sculptural pieces, often of cats, are composed from thrown sections assembled when leatherhard. Norwegian maker Arne Ase is professor of ceramics and an inventive potter who has pioneered the development of techniques such as the use of water soluble metal salts to create a delicate 'water colour' quality to the clay surface of his finely potted bowls. Astrid Gerhartz is a German potter who also makes use of metal salts to colour her translucent cylindrical forms.

Industrial techniques such as slipcasting have found a place in the repertoire of creative makers such as Bodil Manz, a Danish ceramicist who, in collaboration with her husband Richard Manz, developed a unique vision of contemporary porcelain. Her cast forms, with an integrated coloured enamel surface, push porcelain to its structural limits.

Karl Scheid. Thrown and altered form with brown and black glaze.

It is clear that during the last part of the 20th century, there was a rekindling of interest in porcelain as a medium suitable for expressing a huge range of ideas. While much of the work of early studio porcelain makers was purely decorative or ornamental, a new wave of ceramicists has seen the potential of porcelain as a material which could be used to make objects for contemplation or for use. For example in the USA, Akio Takamori uses lightly salt-glazed porcelain as a canvas for his striking vessel-based figurative pieces, merging the boundaries between painting and sculpture. Rebecca Harvey takes ideas from functional forms and invents contemporary objects which have a resonance with the richly coloured porcelains of Europe. The European tradition of modelled figures and figure groups is extended by the work of Michael Flynn. His work in collaboration with some of the major porcelain factories has given him the opportunity to use refined material and technical resources in a personal, creative way. His work introduces contemporary issues and ideas to revitalise a somewhat jaded tradition.

Perhaps one of the most striking recent developments is the way in which some contemporary potters view the austere properties of porcelain as an inspiration for making functional work. The resurgence of interest in minimalism within the wider art, design and fashion world has provided a stage for the work of a number of makers who value the whiteness and tactile qualities of high fired porcelain. Joanna

Constantinidis made a small range of essentially domestic items. Her cups and saucers have an exquisite sense of form and balance, beautifully proportioned, and decorated only with a simple semi-matt glaze. Edmund de Waal has described some of his favourite work as 'Kitchen Porcelain', the simple undecorated mass-produced bowls and dishes used in France. His own thrown, celadon glazed pots are domestic objects, certainly, but with their inherent sense and knowledge of the East, they carry deeper layers of meaning.

Exponents of this new white ware include a group of younger ceramicists recently graduated from art colleges. Hilary Roberts makes thrown and slab-built tableware decorated with relief stamps or subtly differing white glazes. Gilda Westermann throws her forms and decorates them with impressions of shells. Daniel Smith and Karen Downing have both rejected any form of applied surface treatment, relying only on carefully applied glaze.

In the 20th century we saw individual potters grappling with both aesthetic and technical issues, seeking to create clays and glazes which in some way achieved the qualities of those ideals set by Song dynasty potters. We have seen a revolt against the extravagance of rococo opulence, the decline of a trend towards ornament, and the flowering of a movement which values the essence and unadorned beauty of the material. We have also seen porcelain become accepted as a material for contemporary sculpture making. The challenge for contemporary makers is to accept and enjoy the increasing quality and diversity of the materials now available, to produce work which has a clarity of intention and the vision to inspire a new generation of users and collectors.

Jack Doherty. Group of functional porcelain forms. *Photograph by Sue Packer.*

Chapter Three
The Materials

Porcelain clay bodies are made from a relatively small number of basic ceramic materials which are all readily available from pottery suppliers. The ingredients are china clay, feldspar, quartz and a plasticising element such as ball clay, bentonite or an artificial plasticiser, or a combination of both. These are all naturally occurring minerals which are mined and processed for a wide range of industries, from paper-making to cat litter production. Within the ceramics industry each of these materials is available from many sources, for a variety of purposes and providing different qualities. While the choice of particular materials is crucial to the success of a porcelain clay, it is useful to examine each of the materials in a generic sense and to describe their function in the composition of clay bodies.

China clay (Kaolin): $Al_2 O_3\ 2SiO_2\ 2H_2O$

A primary clay, because it is found at the site where it was formed, china clay is the purest clay type containing very little iron oxide or titania. The sequence of events which lead to its development began over 300 million years ago with the formation of granite. The main constituents of granite are feldspar, quartz and mica. While the molten rock was cooling, it was attacked by a succession of liquids and gases including steam, boron and fluorine which, in a complex series of chemical actions, converted the feldspar into china clay.

China clay has a relatively large particle size, and as a result is considerably less plastic than the secondary clays. It is also accepted that the kaolins found in China and other parts of the Far East are more workable than those found in Europe, although there are clays from the USA which have a

The analysis of some commonly used china clays

	SiO_2	Al_2O_3	Fe_2O_3	TiO_2	CaO	$Na_2 O$	$K_2 O$	$KNaO$	S_2O_3	P_2O_5	MgO
Grolleg	47.7	37.7	0.60	0.03	0.10	1.92	0.25				
EPK	46	37.8	0.6	0.40	0.10	0.20	0.25	0.03	0.05	0.15	
No. 6 Tile	46.9	38.2	0.35	1.42	0.43	0.04				0.58	

reasonable plasticity. China clays are mined in many countries including the Czech Republic, England, USA and more recently New Zealand, which is the source of some of the purest clays. China clay is a material high in alumina with an average silica content, making it a refractory clay with a virification point of 1770°C/3218°F. It forms the main clay content of a porcelain body, and is used in quantities of around 50%.

In the UK, the most commonly used china clays for porcelain clay making are Grolleg, Standard Porcelain and Super Standard Porcelain. These are listed in order of increasing fineness, purity and cost. In the USA, Edgar Plastic Kaolin (EPK) and No. 6 Tile are widely used, being relatively white firing and plastic. Zettlitz clays from the Czech Republic are used in the European porcelain industry.

Feldspar: potash feldspar, K_2O Al_2O_3 $6SiO_2$, soda feldspar Na_2O Al_2O_3 $6SiO_2$

The feldspar group of minerals has around 20 members of which nine are common. The most common feldspars are orthoclase (potassium aluminium silicate) and albite (sodium aluminium silicate). In ceramics terms, feldspars are natural frits or glazes containing silica, alumina and alkalis.

Orthoclase is the pure mineral. The material available to potters is potash feldspar which will contain small quantities of other feldspars. Potash feldspar will melt at approximately 1200°C/2192°F to produce an opaque stiff glass. It has a high alumina content and a long melting period which allows vitrification to occur over a wide temperature range. Potash feldspar is the most commonly used flux in the manufacture of porcelain bodies.

Albite or soda feldspar can also be used as a body flux. It has more powerful fluxing properties than potash feldspar and will operate over a shorter temperature range. It will begin to volatilize at 1200°C/2192°F. Different colour responses can be expected if albite is used in place of orthoclase.

Other feldspathic materials which can be used as fluxes are Cornish stone and nepheline syenite. Cornish stone melts at a higher temperature range than potash or soda feldspar, from 1250°C–1350°C/ 2282°–2462°F, raising the maturing point of the body. Nepheline syenite melts in the range 1100°C–1200°C/ 2012°–2192°F and can be used to replace part of the feldspar content, lowering the firing temperature of the clay.

Quartz (silica): SiO_2

Silica is the most important glass former. It adds hardness and durability to clay bodies, and is obtained from quartz rock, flint or silica sand. Silica has a melting point of 1710°C/3110°F and must be used in conjunction with a flux. In porcelain clay bodies, flint or quartz are used in amounts of between 15% and 25%. As with all of the materials used in porcelain making, care must be taken to select those which are free from impurity, particularly iron oxide.

Ball clay

Ball clays are secondary clays which have been moved from their source by the effects of weathering and erosion. Janet and Frank Hamer describe ball clays as 'once removed kaolins'. These are clays which contain a high proportion of kaolinite – the pure clay mineral – but which have collected impurities in the form of alkalis, titanium and iron. There are a huge number of ball clays available which have a wide range of individual characteristics.

They are highly plastic clays which generally fire to a light colour. They have a vitrification range of between 1100°C –1200°C/2012–2192°F. Ball clays have a small particle size which accounts for their plasticity, the main quality which they add to porcelain clay bodies. An addition of around 10% will produce a significant improvement in plasticity and increased dry strength. These virtues must be balanced, however, against their high shrinkage and their detrimental effect on purity and colour.

Bentonite: Al_2O_3 $4SiO_2$ H_2O

Bentonite is a member of the group of montmorillonite silicates which were formed from the decomposition of volcanic ash. In many ways a material with extraordinary properties, it has uses in many industries, from well drilling to cat litter production.

The key to its usefulness to porcelain makers lies in its molecular structure. It has a layered structure resembling a 'stack' of clay platelets. Unlike other clays there are no hydroxyl bonds holding the platelets together, and as a result they are able to slide over one another. Because there is no bond linking the layers, water can penetrate and separate the platelets. Bentonite can absorb ten times its weight in water and can swell by up to 18 times its dry volume. While bentonite has obvious advantages for the clay maker, there are some drawbacks. It contains iron which has a detrimental effect on the fired colour of the porcelain. Lighter burning bentonites can be found, for example the Quest white bentonite which was successfully used in the production of the David Leach clay. Found in the Mediterranean region, formed by the action of sea water on volcanic ash, it is a calcium bentonite with a high montmorillonite content (giving high plasticity) and low iron. It is soda-activated to improve its gelling qualities. Bentonite is used in amounts up to 5%. It can be used as the only plasticising material or in combination with ball clay.

Macalloid

Macalloid is a plasticising material derived from hectorite, a montmorillonitic ore. It is preferred to bentonite by some potters, as it has a lower iron content and is therefore less likely to affect the clay body colour.

Vee Gum T

A Macalloid type suspension agent which can be used to suspend glazes or as an aid to plasticity in clay bodies.

Chapter Four
Porcelain Bodies

Unlike most stoneware and earthenware clay bodies which can be single, naturally occurring clays or blends of natural clays, porcelain is a material which, in the West, is a manufactured material. In the West, the essential qualities of purity and whiteness and translucency so valued by potters and collectors depend on the use of comparatively non-plastic materials, the kaolins available in Europe being generally less workable than those found in China and Japan. This is not a problem when producing clays for industrial methods such as slipcasting, but studio potters require clays for throwing and handbuilding. These processes demand a degree of plasticity so there has been a great deal of pioneering research by individual potters and manufacturers to develop clays suitable for hand production.

In *A Potters Book*, Bernard Leach gives the recipe of the St Ives porcelain body as:

Varcoes No.1 china clay	45
Varcoes water ground feldspar	25
Pikes siliceous ball clay	16.66
Wengers water ground quartz	13.33

Lucie Rie used a variation of this recipe:

China clay	45
Feldspar	25
Ball clay	8.33
Flint	13.33
Bentonite	8.33

She mixed the clay by hand in fairly small amounts, sometimes using soda feldspar which produces a brighter colour response in some of her glazes. It is a clay dependant on an addition of ball clay for plasticity and workability. As a result it is a body which resembles porcelainous stoneware. It is interesting to compare this clay with the one developed by David Leach and marketed since the early 1970s. His recipe is:

Standard porcelain china clay	52
Potash feldspar	25
200's mesh quartz	20
Quest white bentonite	3

In the search for a purer, whiter body, the plasticising ball clay content has been replaced by bentonite.

Commercially produced porcelain clay bodies

Relatively few studio porcelain makers are prepared to spend the time and effort needed to produce their own clay. Peter Lane expresses a commonly held view, 'I've not made my porcelain for many years because it is so much easier to buy ready-prepared clay and have more time for making.' Most of the potters I questioned have found a clay which suits their making methods from those commercially available. In recent years clay manufacturers have increased both the range and quality of their porcelain bodies. There are currently at least 15 porcelains available in the UK, offering a very wide range of making and firing possibilities. There are many more available in the USA and Australia. For example, the Clay Art Center in Tacone, Washington, alone offers 14 different porcelains with a range of firing temperatures from cone 4 to cone 11. 'Southern Ice' porcelain, developed by Les Blakeborough and produced by the Walker Clay Company in Australia, is now being exported to many countries. It is a clay of exceptional whiteness and translucency. It has been described by Peter Lane as 'the most exciting porcelain clay I have ever used'.

The choice of clay is crucial to all potters, and porcelain makers have very specific requirements. Joanna Howells uses the high temperature Limoges clay, 'because it has such marvellous throwing qualities. For me this is pre-eminently

Janet DeBoos. Tea cup and saucer. Height: 10 cm (4 in.).

important because of the way I distort the freshly thrown pieces'. The particular qualities of Valentine's 'Audrey Blackman' porcelain are exploited by Margaret O'Rorke in her translucent thrown forms. She writes, 'I have chosen this clay because it has been developed specifically for its translucency. I found it responsive to the touch, plastic and versatile when thrown thinly. It can withstand 1300°C/ 2372°F and above. I have not found all these qualities in any other porcelain body which I have used in the UK, Japan, Australia or the USA'. But a single clay may not meet all of the requirements of individual potters. Both Julian Stair and Caroline Whyman use a 50:50 blend of Potclays HF 1149 and Valentine's 'Audrey Blackman'. Julian claims that both throw very well, 'HF1149 is good for constructing but the glaze fit is not so good; Valentine's AB is very white but has a tendency to crack. When mixed in equal amounts they cancel out each others negative characteristics'.

I use three clays for their differing qualities. I use 'Audrey Blackman' to make small fine translucent cups and bowls, because of its outstanding whiteness. When thinly thrown it is perfectly translucent. Larger forms are made using high temperature Limoges porcelain which is designed to fire to 1400°C/2552°F. It is essentially a stable clay when fired at cone 10 and in my experience less likely to develop firing cracks. It also can produce a beautiful lustrous surface when fired in my soda kiln. I make a production range of functional pieces, tea bowls, cups and saucers etc and for these I use Potclays HF 1149. It is an excellent general purpose material, less translucent than the others but with a good fired colour.

Clay production

Few clay manufacturers have a dedicated porcelain making plant, but changing to porcelain production involves an extensive cleaning operation. Harry Fraser at Potclays talked of a three day change over period when blungers, pugmill and slip lines were stripped down and thoroughly washed. Good housekeeping and stringent cleanliness are essential to avoid contamination from iron bearing clays and materials which are being produced elsewhere in the factory.

Most porcelain clay bodies are produced using traditional sliphouse methods. The dry ingredients are mixed with water, turned into slop form and then combined in carefully measured amounts in a blunger. This blunging or mixing time is important. Longer mixing produces a finer material and consequently a more plastic clay body. Ball milling will produce a clay of an even finer particle size and plasticity. However, only small quantities can be made and production times are longer. After the initial mixing, the impure porcelain slip is sieved through a 180–200s mesh. This refinement continues as the slip is passed over a powerful electromagnet and then over a rare earth magnet cluster. This stage of

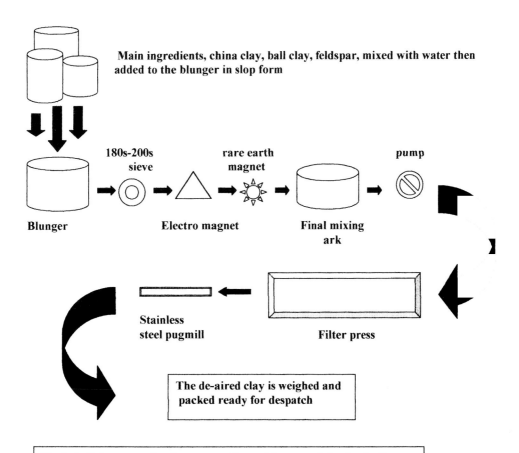

Main ingredients, china clay, ball clay, feldspar, mixed with water then added to the blunger in slop form

180s-200s sieve

rare earth magnet

pump

Blunger

Electro magnet

Final mixing ark

Stainless steel pugmill

Filter press

The de-aired clay is weighed and packed ready for despatch

Typical sliphouse production process for making porcelain clay bodies

29

the process is designed to remove all of the iron particles from the clay. The refined slip is collected in a final ark before being pumped at around 200psi into a filter press.

This is the 'de-watering' phase of production where the clay slip is turned into a plastic body. The slip is forced under pressure through a series of fabric filters known as cloths. The excess water drips away, leaving the clay behind in the form of flat filter cakes. The pressing time can vary considerably. The higher quality clays made from finer materials will take longer than the 'economy' porcelains. (Alan Ault of Valentine's Clays describes a pressing time of five hours for their P2 body, and eight hours for the Audrey Blackman.) The clay body is then passed through a stainless steel de-airing pugmill, before being carefully weighed and packed into polythene bags. The

Clay loops, air drying.

most common pack sizes available in the UK are 12.5 and 25 kg bags. The French Limoges bodies are sold in 20 kg packs. The consistency at which clays are packed and sold is often controversial. Clay suppliers sometimes use a penetration meter to gauge the consistency of their products, a simple device for measuring the clay's hardness. The relative measure used is the NGK scale, calibrated from 0 to 20. It is not a perfect system as in practice a degree of tolerance will creep in and clays will be described as having hardness of 5 to 6. Potters have strong opinions and specific individual requirements. For my own work I prefer clay which has lost its 'stickiness' and feels firm. To achieve this state it is usually necessary to open the fresh bags and to allow the clay to air dry. I do this by slicing the clay and bending it into 'loops' which allows the air to circulate freely. This process can be speeded up by placing the clay loops

outside in dry weather, taking care to avoid contamination from dust, leaves and gravel.

Clay producers do listen to the views and ideas of potters and have made porcelain bodies for individual makers. They deal with a demanding clientele. When asked if she made her own clay, Caroline Whyman replied, 'No, I have no space to do this, but would if I could. I think that commercial bodies in general are not allowed to sour and age, and these processes are vital to create a really plastic, throwable porcelain clay.'

Designing and making a porcelain body in relatively small quantities is not technically difficult, but if it is to be produced regularly for a studio scale production it will require space, organization and planning.

Clay making in the studio

Formulating a clay body for use in the studio will almost certainly involve compromise. A general porcelain recipe which uses common materials is easy to devise but will need adjustment and fine tuning. The choice of the basic range of raw materials is straightforward. We know that kaolin or China clay is the low iron bearing clay available to potters. It is a relatively non-plastic clay, so an addition of a plasticising material such as ball clay or bentonite will be necessary. China clays are high in alumina and therefore refractory, with a vitrification point of around 1770°C/3218°F. Fluxes need to be added to make them mature within a chosen temperature range. Feldspar contains the required fluxes, and is readily available and inexpensive. Flint is used to reduce body expansion making it easier to fit glazes. It is also an inexpensive filler and firing stabilizer.

The following are some of the physical properties which many porcelain makers would consider to be important features of a clay body:

Translucency In order to be translucent, the clay must have a low level of light absorption, caused by the presence of metal ions. In practice this means using clays which contain as little iron or titanium oxides as possible.

Whiteness Again dependent on the factors of light absorption and light scatter. Light scatter is caused by crystalline materials which reflect a proportion of light as it passes through. Again choice of materials is important. Kaolins, ball clays and bentonites can all contain iron which will affect the purity of the fired porcelain.

Workability Choices can be made depending on the forming processes to be used. As an example, throwing clays will require plasticity. Achieving a reasonable throwing body will involve compromise and the use of materials detrimental to the fired colour. The cleanest materials are the least plastic so that casting clays can be made with much less compromise achieving purer, whiter and more translucent results.

Glaze fit Balancing the quartz content of the body is an important factor in achieving a stable clay. Too little quartz can mean that glazes will craze. Quartz assists low expansion, helping glaze fit. Too much quartz can lower plasticity and can cause problems with dunting.

Making a porcelain body in the studio

Experimental clays and small batches can be made in the studio by replicating some of the sliphouse methods used by the manufacturers. The following body recipe is a good starting point for a porcelain to be fired at cone 9. Experiment with different types of china clay or ball clay and china clay combinations.

China clay	50
Potash feldspar	25
Silica	25
Bentonite	2

The equipment needed

An accurate scales, two large plastic dustbins, sieves from 60s to 200s mesh; a power mixer will speed up the process but is not essential. It is important to stress that all of the equipment and utensils and work surfaces must be clean. Health and Safety issues must also be considered. Care must always be taken when working with fine powdered materials. Silica, whether in the form of flint, quartz or as a part of feldspar or clay dust is a particular hazard. Wear a suitable mask. Take care when opening sacks of powdered materials. Clean up using a wet sponge or mop.

Half fill one of the bins with water. Weigh the china clay and add this to water, mixing thoroughly, weigh and add the feldspar followed by the silica. Bentonite and other plasticisers such as macalloid are difficult to add to clay bodies. They absorb large quantities of water and form a glutinous gel. Mix the bentonite with at least twice its volume of water and soak overnight. Sieve the plasticiser into the clay mixture and allow the materials to soak for at least 24 hours. The ingredients should then be carefully mixed – a power mixer is useful – speeding up the process and producing a finer, more plastic clay. The mixture is then sieved into the second bin. Commercial clays are sieved through a 200s mesh power sieve, but it is easier to achieve this in the studio by using a series of sieves from 60s to 200s. The completed slip is allowed to settle before the excess water is poured away. The resulting material must then be dried to a plastic consistency, which can be done in a variety of ways. If the slip is very thin it can be poured into a de-watering tray, where the excess water slowly drips away. The thickened slip can then be stiffened on plaster slabs. I prefer to use thickly thrown shallow bisque bowls, as these avoid the risk of plaster contamination.

It is worth taking care not to allow a hard crust to form on one side of the drying clay, avoidable by turning the clay regularly. It can also help to cover the plaster slab or bisque bowl with a clean cloth first.

The clay must now be wedged or kneaded, wrapped tightly in clean polythene and stored before use. This ageing and souring process plays an important part in producing a plastic and workable clay body. Ageing is a physical action which allows the slow penetration of water between the clay particles, this produces more particles of a smaller size.

Souring involves an organic action. As bacteria break down organic matter in the clay, amino acids are released which flocculate the mineral particles. Flocculated particles are attracted to one another, giving the clay greater strength. Soured clay often smells like rotting vegetation – a good sign. During ageing, the clay is slowly compressed under its own weight. This action again has the effect of forcing the clay part-icles closer together, increasing work-ability. The effects of compression can be simulated by wedging or, ideally, using a de-airing pugmill. The longer a clay is aged the better, although it is unlikely that contemporary potters will make clays for their descendants as was the practice in China. For us, three months would probably be the minimum effective period for ageing clay. Ideally clay should be stored in cool and damp conditions – a cellar with a stable temperature would be a perfect but not easily attainable solution. It should be protected from extreme temperature changes and it should be stored in a wetter condition than that needed for throwing.

Porcelain clays can be modified with the addition of other materials in order to solve specific making problems. The addition of Molochite can help reduce warping and distortion caused by high shrinkage. Molochite is essentially a calcined china clay and is used as a refractory white grog. It is available in a number of grades and can be wedged or kneaded into small amounts of the porcelain body. Amounts from 10 to 20% are common.

Modellers and sculptors have found that a small addition of nylon or polyester fibre will increase the workability of the clay giving added strength in the wet state. Adding 0.5% will provide a matrix of fibres which will allow the clay to be worked extremely thinly and into complicated shapes without cracking. Colin Pearson uses this method to make the complex and delicate 'wings' which are added to his vessel forms. If too much fibre is added it can adversely affect the fired strength of the work. Other materials such as white cotton fibre or shredded denim can be successfully used to add interesting textures. David Maybin of Scarva Pottery Supplies in Ireland has produced a range of sculptural bodies (including a porcelain) which contain flax fibre.

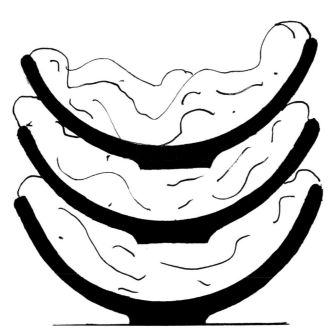

Thickly thrown biscuit fired bowls can be used as an alternative to plaster bats.

Porcelain clay recipes

Cone 9		Cone 11	
China clay	50.6	China clay	51
Feldspar	28.1	Ball clay	7
Silica	15.7	Feldspar	18
Bentonite	5.6	Silica	24

Cone 8		Cone 8/9	
China clay	40	China clay	50
Ball clay	9	Feldspar	27
Silica	18	Silica	17
Nepheline syenite	31	Whiting	1
Bentonite	2	Bentonite	5

Cone 9/10		Cone 9	
China clay	54	China clay	42
Feldspar	25	Silica	22
Silica	25	Feldspar	33
Bentonite	5	Bentonite	2

Modifying clays with paper pulp is a relatively recent phenomenon. Porcelain bodies can be mixed with paper pulp. Paper clay allows complex forms to be constructed with a great deal of freedom. For example it is possible to break all the conventional rules about joining. Clay can be assembled at any stage of dryness or with wet sections joined to dry, or even added to biscuit-fired clay. The ratio of clay to paper pulp can be varied, 1 part of pulp (by volume) to four parts of porcelain clay slurry is a good starting point. While paper pulp can be made by shredding and soaking tissue or newspaper etc., the process can be speeded up by purchasing cellulose and other fibres directly from a pottery materials supplier (see list of suppliers on p.109).

Chapter Five
Forming Methods and Problem-solving

Porcelain forms can be made using every known technique, with inventive makers continuously developing ways of using porcelain clay, exploiting its special properties. Porcelain clays have, of course, their own characteristics. Each clay will behave differently, and should be selected for its ability to respond to the demands of a specific technique. When choosing a clay for a particular process it is important to test several different bodies from a number of manufacturers. Make sure that you have enough clay to complete a number of pieces. Making and firing small tests will provide very little information. Also make pieces of various different sizes. Some clays which are very suitable for small scale work may show a range of faults when used on a large scale.

Handbuilding

The most simple techniques can be used to great effect. Pinch forms have been made by many potters as the starting point for interesting porcelain works. It is also an excellent way of gauging the working properties of a clay. Making a pot from a ball of clay simply by hollowing it out with the fingers demands concentration and skill. Open up the ball of clay with the thumb, slowly turning the ball. Pinch the walls of the pot slowly and rhythmically, stretching and thinning the clay. As the form becomes thinner, it can be

Opening a ball of clay with the thumb.

Pinching and refining the form.

supported with sponge or foam. The form will always tend to open as the work progresses, so care is needed to prevent the clay from sagging and collapsing. Coils or strips can be added to increase the size of the pot.

Basic forms can be refined and developed using tools such as metal and plastic scrapers, hacksaw blades and

Smoothing and scraping the surface with a metal kidney.

kitchen knives. It is also useful to adapt tools designed for other materials. There are many types of wood or plastic cutting blades, for example the 'surform', which make very effective clay tools.

Working with coils can be seen as a technique on its own, or as a way of extending work begun by pinching. Care should be taken to ensure sound joins, making sure that the clay is of equal consistency.

Slab-building can be an exciting and versatile way of working with porcelain. The slabs can be used at the leatherhard stage for making precise angular forms, or they can be used in a much wetter state, rolled or stretched for shapes which have a softer character. Most porcelain clay slabs will tend to warp if not treated carefully during making. They should be carefully made on a slightly absorbent surface and then dried slowly until the correct consistency is achieved. Avoid making slabs on shiny surfaces such as plastic laminates, since the clay will stick to this material, cracking as it dries and shrinks. An addition of Molochite can be kneaded into the body, helping reduce shrinkage to produce more stable slabs. Experiment

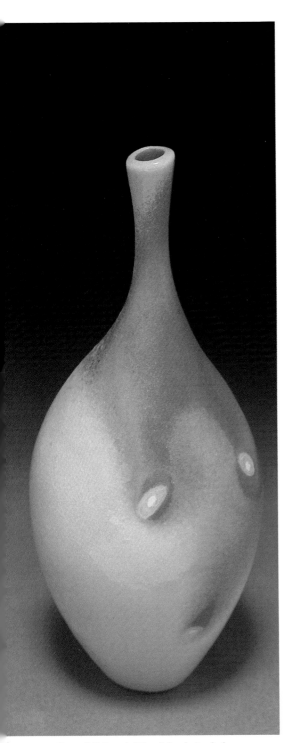
Joyce Michaud. Wood-fired pinch form.

Right
Jack Doherty. Wire cut and stretched slab.

Below
A coloured agate clay block.
Bottom
The block sliced to show matching surfaces.

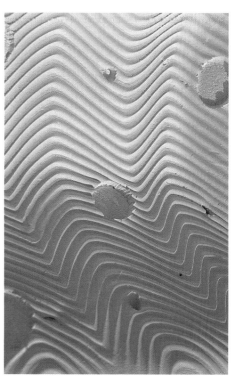

Taking care to compress the bevelled, scored and slipped joints.

with amounts from 5–10%. A disadvantage is that even the finest grades of Molochite will alter the surface quality of the material. It will also change the workability of the body, making the clay 'short' and more likely to crack during the making process. As with all porcelain techniques, joining must be done with care.

Joining porcelain

Clays which are extremely fine textured, containing no sand or grog can be difficult to join securely. Porcelain bodies are very tight and dense and do not absorb water easily at the leatherhard stage, so that extra effort must be made to make sure that the surfaces to be joined have been well scored and softened. Porcelain makers have developed many ways of coping with joining problems. The single most important factor is to ensure that the pieces to be joined are of equal consistency. It means being in control of drying, difficult enough in the studio but much harder for students in colleges. It may be worthwhile devising damp environments for the storage of porcelain pieces in progress. Large plastic storage boxes containing a damp sponge can be used to keep handles and lids, etc. in workable

Joan Doherty. Group of unglazed slab-built agate boxes.

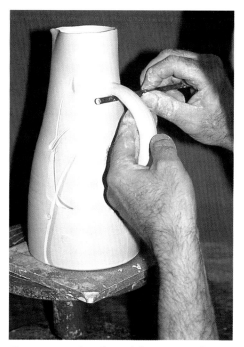

Handles must be securely joined. The handles have been pulled and allowed to dry to the same consistency as the pot.

Compressing the edges of the join – with a wooden modelling tool can help to prevent cracks.

condition for a long period. Some potters have used discarded fridges or freezers to create airtight damp cupboards. Often it is necessary to improvise, using clean polythene and tape, constructing a temporary framework to protect the soft work.

The most common method of joining clay is to scratch or score both of the surfaces to be joined, then apply water or slip and press the pieces together, manipulating them if possible to ensure a good joint. Remember that the joint is formed by 'welding' the surface together with pressure, not relying on slip as a glue. Some potters prefer using vinegar instead of water or slip; it will act quickly on the porcelain, dissolving and softening the clay. Joining liquids or pastes may also be used.

Joining liquid: added to one gallon of water
3 tablespoons sodium silicate
5 g soda ash

Joining paste
Clay body	1 kg
Feldspar	20 g
Bentonite	20 g
Gum Arabic	20 g

Mix the dry materials, then measure 500 cc of water and add 5 cc of powerful liquid deflocculant such as Dispex to the water (Darvan 7 is a similar product in the USA). Stir the dry mixture into the water to make a slip. Re-flocculate with a small amount of Epsom salts in solution.

Porcelain clays have a high shrinkage – 15% is common. This is a factor in causing cracks where the clay has been joined. Uneven drying will also stress joints and cause cracking during firing. Where possible drying should be done slowly and evenly – protecting the work from draughts or excessive heat.

The wheel

Throwing with porcelain is a favourite making method of studio potters. Most commercially produced clays will perform well on the wheel. But it is worth testing several by throwing a variety of forms with each. It is also worth remembering that with most things we get what we pay for. The more expensive bodies are made from high quality ingredients demanding increased manufacturing time and higher cost.

The clay itself is pleasant to use, with a smooth sensuous feel. It does, however, have particular characteristics which must be considered. As with all clays, preparation is crucial. It is frustrating to try to work with clay which contains air pockets or is the wrong consistency. It is important to check the clay consistency

well in advance of a throwing session. Porcelain clays, especially those containing bentonite, will absorb water during the throwing, rapidly softening the form. I have found that using firmer clay will provide some respite against sudden collapse of the pot. If using a commercial clay, open the bags as the clay may need to be air dried. I avoid rapidly drying the clay on materials such as plaster which will have a detrimental effect on the plasticity of the body. Whilst I must confess to using clay

Compressing the centre of the base can help to prevent cracks developing during drying.

Coning the clay as part of the centring will help to eliminate unevenness.

Throwing with a small wet sponge will lubricate the clay and spread finger pressure.

A flexible rubber kidney is a useful tool for smoothing the inside of open forms.

A straight edged tool like a hacksaw blade can be used to refine the exterior surface.

Compressing the rim with a sponge or rib can prevent cracking and distortion.

straight from a de-airing pugmill for small pieces, I would recommend that porcelain should be thoroughly kneaded before throwing. I spiral knead on a wooden surface (a strong pine table bought from an army surplus store) which is slightly absorbent. Other surfaces such as slate or slabs made from polished concrete will provide a functional surface. Basic preparation before a throwing session would include checking and cleaning tools and equipment, vital if other clays are used in the workshop. Attitudes to cleanliness vary: if Margaret O'Rorke uses a different clay then 'cleaning becomes a surgical process'. Janet DeBoos also uses a porcellaneous stoneware for her production work, 'I'm not looking for the purity that many porcelain workers are. I don't mind a bit of grot, as long as it is acceptable grot!'

The principles of throwing porcelain are no different from any other clay. Many of the problems which are associated with using porcelain on the wheel arise from not recognising the individual qualities of the clay and by using it in the same way and for the same forms as earthenware or stoneware. Successful thrown porcelain forms depend on an understanding of structure. The shapes must be designed with sufficient clay in the right places to withstand the sometimes dramatic changes which happen during drying and firing. With stoneware or earthenware clays it is possible to disguise weakness or unevenness, but any flaws in porcelain will be revealed mercilessly during the firing. Remember that porcelain bodies will differ in their capacity to withstand 'rough treatment'. Some are best when thrown thickly and then refined by turning or trimming. Lucie Rie's bowls are an outstanding

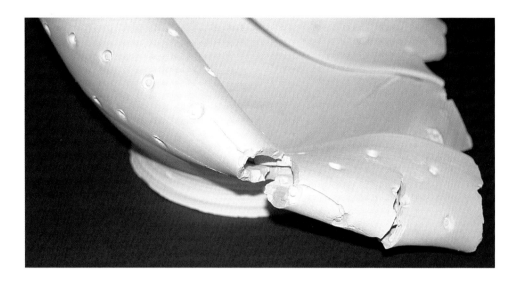

A weakened rim can cause a dramatic collapse.

example of how these techniques can be used creatively. Her sensitive use of tools and her understanding of the nature of the material are revealed in forms of great subtlety.

Lucie Rie often used improvised tools such as an 'old fashioned' razor blade to hone and refine her work. The results however were never mechanical; her pots capture and distill the life and movement of the wheel.

While the principles of throwing remain essentially the same as for other clays, porcelain makers often evolve individual approaches and processes to deal with some of the less forgiving features of the material. I find it more convenient and efficient to throw all my work on bats. It helps to minimise distortion caused by lifting freshly thrown pots from the wheel. Bats are particularly useful when making fine open bowls which are easily damaged in the soft state. They can be purchased from pottery suppliers, several different systems being available, or they can be

made in the studio. A good quality marine plywood is a suitable material for bats. Choose a thickness approximately 12mm thick, which will ensure that the bats are rigid and will not flex when prised from the wheel. Even small uncontrolled movements such as this can cause unwanted distortion or collapse delicate forms. It is important that they are kept in good condition. Bats which have become warped or have eneven surfaces can make working with small or fine forms difficult.

Porcelain is a 'thirsty' clay. It absorbs water quickly, which can lead to sudden collapse of the forms. Paradoxically it also needs to remain well lubricated. Margaret O'Rorke is one of a number of potters who use a gas burner to stiffen work during the throwing. It is important not to allow either the clay or the hands to become dry. A dry finger can easily drag on the work, causing a dramatic collapse. It is possible to throw with slip but I find that it makes it difficult to judge the thickness of thin pieces. I sometimes throw with a wet sponge held in one hand. It is a useful technique, especially for large forms, as it continually lubricates the clay and allows greater pressure to be applied without causing deep finger marks.

Base cracks can be a common and annoying fault with many porcelain clays. It is essential not to allow work to begin to dry and shrink on a bat or work board. Make sure that the pots have been 'wired,' or are placed on an absorbent surface. Some makers use a layer of newspaper. 'S' cracks usually occur as a result of unequal shrinkage between the walls and base of the pot. An adjustment of your throwing technique can often help to minimise these. It can help to apply additional compression to the clay, first by coning during centring and then by applying extra finger pressure to the base of the pot, running the fingers from the centre to the outside several times. It also makes sense not to leave pools of water standing on the inside of the pot. Remove excess water with a sponge on a stick. As with most porcelain making processes, attention to detail can prevent problems occurring at a later stage.

Thrown and altered form

Thrown forms are often used as a starting point for more complex work. Squeezing soft thrown pots is probably the simplest and one of the most apposite methods of changing the character of wheel-made porcelain. Many makers use this method to produce subtle ovoid forms. Prue Venables makes pots which have left behind the roundness of thrown work but which in their reformed state still carry the mark of the wheel.

Experiment with other ways of applying pressure to the work. Pieces of wood or sponge can be used to give particular effects. It may be necessary to begin altering the form when the clay is soft, but then return to give the shape more definition as the work begins to dry. Be cautious about applying pressure to the rims of thin pieces, as most porcelain clays will crack easily. It is

Daniel Fisher. Thrown and manipulated form.

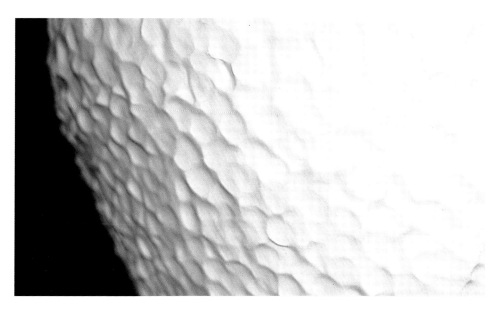

especially vulnerable when it has dried beyond the leatherhard state. Cracks which begin at the rim are extremely difficult to repair and will invariably open up during the firing.

Porcelain will shrink at a higher rate than most other clays, a feature which can cause distortion – a nuisance to many potters, but this is a characteristic which can be exploited. Subtle and gentle shapes can be produced by cutting away the rim of thrown and altered forms and then allowing the work to dry and shrink, changing shape as it does. These shapes can be enhanced as the pots shrink further in the kiln.

Ruthanne Tudball throws and then alters her work as soon as the throwing is complete, carving and faceting with a cheese cutter, the cuts sharp and fluid, describing the nature of the wet clay. Daniel Fisher manipulates and alters his thrown forms by hanging them from an upside down turntable and pulling and stretching them from the inside. He pinches and drags the clay, exploiting its plasticity.

Using a fine hardwood rib to trim excess clay from the base of a deep bowl.

Squaring a thrown form with a wooden block.

A thrown bowl squeezed and manipulated into an oval form.

Levelling the top of the squared form.

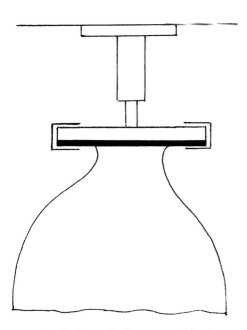

Daniel Fisher's upside-down turntable; the work is thrown on bats which are then clipped to the turntable.

Composite forms

Most advanced throwing techniques can be used with porcelain clays. Large pieces can be made by throwing and joining sections or by adding and throwing coils. Care should be taken when joining sections – ideally the consistency of the clay should be as similar as possible to help prevent the joints pulling apart as the work dries. The pieces should also be dried slowly and carefully to help prevent uneven shrinkage. I prefer to make large pieces by adding thrown rings to the base section. It is always worth taking extra care to make sure that the joins are secure before beginning to throw.

Top Adding a thrown section to a leatherhard base. Both sections are slipped and scored.
Centre The edges must be securely sealed.
Bottom Throwing the added section.

Tools for throwing porcelain

Group of fine hardwood throwing ribs.

All throwers will have their favourite tools. Often they have been developed from traditional models or modified to perform particular tasks. There are an enormous number of these commercially available and it is worth taking time to try out a range of different tools, to discover those that are comfortable to use and that really work. Tools can be seen as extensions of the hands, designed to perform special tasks, and the most effective can sometimes be borrowed or adapted from another role. Porcelain clays and the forms produced from it have special qualities. Its dense, smooth and fine grained quality demands a sharpness in tools which is not usually necessary for working other clays. I use a series of hardwood throwing ribs which are smaller than the conventional ones. I have these made with sharper angles and edges, giving greater control and precision when cutting into the sticky wet clay.

Cutting wires are usually designed for use with coarser materials; a three- or five-strand twisted wire can drag through the base of finer porcelain forms and may even distort the rims of small pieces. I make cutting wires for small work by unravelling a conventional wire and using just one strand, which makes a much sharper and more effective tool for working with porcelain.

The sponge is an important part of a thrower's tool kit. I use a number of different types, from small natural sponges to the more coarse-grained man-made variety, useful for adding a fine texture to the surface of thrown pots. Small, shaped, cosmetic sponges are useful for finishing delicate rims and edges. A sponge on a stick is a commonplace throwing tool; I make a number of sizes to use with a range of different size forms.

Many of my most useful and indispensable tools have been found, adapted or borrowed from other sources.

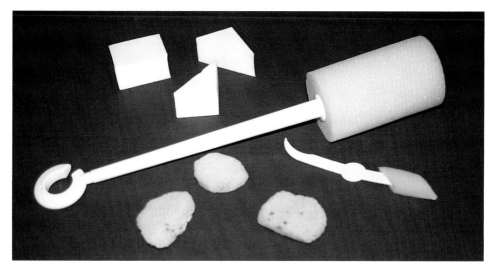

Turning and finishing

Found tools 1; cosmetic and cleaning sponges.

Refinement, thinness and precision are some of the classic porcelain qualities which are often achieved through various post-throwing processes. Turning or trimming is frequently used as a method of achieving thinness and translucency. Sensitively done, it can be used to develop some of the unique qualities of the material, badly used it can destroy the life and movement of the form. Porcelain is a seductive material to work with at the leatherhard stage. It is smooth and fine grained, cuts cleanly and is enjoyable to turn. But as with the throwing it is important to have a clear sense of the form and its structure. Weakness caused by thin spots will destroy the work during the firing. Before starting any turning process it is worth spending a little time assessing the piece being worked on, checking the thickness of the clay, its dryness, and being aware of the particular quality which you are trying to achieve. As all of my work is thrown on bats I have found it useful to begin any turning with the pots still attached to the bat. It is liberating to make decisions about pieces when they are the 'right way up'. As it dries, porcelain becomes increasingly vulnerable to damage. I avoid placing pots directly onto the wheelhead for turning. Instead I use a series of 'chucks' improvised from plastic containers. I have a number of different sizes which are filled with clay. A ring of soft clay or a pad of sponge can be added to protect the interior of the work. These make centring and turning thin, fragile forms much easier, the pots are placed on the chuck which is tap centred and then

Large open forms can be left attached to the bat.

47

Trimming excess clay in the upright position.

Improvised chuck using a plastic container filled with clay. A clay coil is added to cushion the pot.

Turning thin forms on chucks will prevent cracking and damage to rims.

Turning on a pad of soft clay.

pegged with clay. This is a flexible way of working, allowing altered asymmetrical forms to be centred. It is also relatively straightforward to remove the work to check for thickness during the process.

Tools

The choice of turning tools is a very personal one. Again there are many types commercially available. Choices

should be made depending on the clay consistency, the size of the form and the finished quality. Steel loop tools will work well with soft clay, while shaped tools are excellent for turning foot rings and for more precise work. Many porcelain makers prefer to use stainless steel tools. They will not rust and contaminate the clay but they can be difficult to keep sharp. If tools are kept well and properly maintained then mild

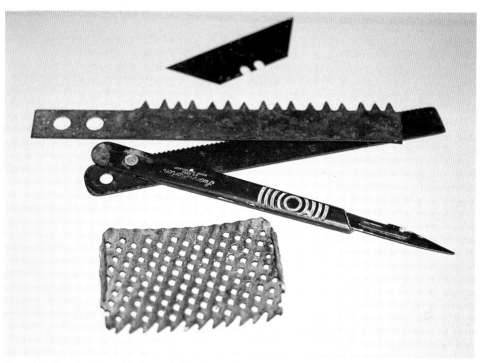

Found tools 2; hacksaw blades and shaping tools.

Found tools 3; paint scraper, pastry cutter and comb.

Using a paint brush to pull the lip on a fine-rimmed jug.

steel is acceptable.

Look around for alternative tools. I use pastry or cookie cutters as turning tools – they are made from very thin sharp steel, are flexible, and can be bent to fit different shapes. There are many types of wood and plastic shaping tools available which work well with porcelain. Tools must be kept sharp – it is surprising how quickly a fine porcelain will blunt tools. Use an electric grinder, oilstone or file before each turning session.

Handbuilt and thrown work can be refined and finished in many ways, and for this there are dedicated scrapers and finishing tools available. Porcelain forms can be completed by scraping, even sandpapering at the biscuit stage, polishing and sandblasting. Look again for effective tools which can be borrowed from other sources. It is worth mentioning that all siliceous materials must be treated with care. The dust from dry porcelain is a health hazard and working practices must take this into account. Avoid generating large quantities of dust and always wear a suitable dust mask.

Slipcasting

Whilst it is essentially an industrial production technique, slipcasting is used creatively by a number of individual porcelain makers. It has some advantages as a porcelain technique, particularly as it allows control of thickness, enabling makers to exploit translucency to a greater degree than might be possible with throwing or handbuilding. Amongst the disadvantages is the investment in time and money necessary for mould making. Pieter Stockmans is both an industrial designer and an artist. His work has its roots in the factory but he uses industrial processes to make art works with references to ceramic production, using multiple images, industrial crockery and so on.

Slipcasting is a viable technique in a small studio. Small-scale blungers and mixing equipment are easily available, making it possible to produce casting slips which can be highly refined.

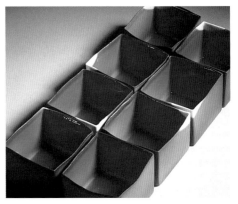

Pieter Stockmans. Slipcast forms.

Chapter Six
Decoration, from Wet Clay to Enamel

The nature of porcelain, the material itself, with its smooth and seductive surface qualities can entrance and intimidate. To become involved with any form of surface decoration demands that the maker be prepared to take risks. Just as making a pencil mark on a fresh sketchbook page can seem daunting, the thought of touching, marking and changing a fresh porcelain surface can inhibit. Porcelain clay is extremely receptive and will show the smallest mark, whether intentional or not. So surface decoration can begin as the forms are being made. Janet DeBoos writes, 'Decorating is by the act of throwing. I want to capture the fresh wetness of just thrown clay'. Her fingers mark and change her pots, softly, with the movement of the wheel. She uses a gas torch to stiffen the form during throwing, preserving the freshness of the surface. The dynamics of the wheel itself are evident in the porcelain works of Japanese potter Ryoji Koie. His spontaneously thrown bowls and cups are often decorated with an incised line, precise and sharp, but drawn with great freedom.

Edmund de Waal applies seal marks to many of his pots. These are marks which alter the form of the work, making small indentations and crevices to be touched and explored in use. They also become a key to understanding the nature and condition of the clay, sensing its softness. The stamps are carved from soapstone, glass or ivory. 'Ancient Japanese pots always had text on them although the characters or texts which I use are illegible to other people. It is a conversation with myself'.

Stamps and seals can be made or found. I use a number of found objects such as discarded jewellery, wood screws and broken paintbrush handles to make the small studs which I press into my pots while they are still wet.

Working directly with soft wet porcelain clay, especially when it is freshly thrown can be challenging but also very satisfying. The clay can be extremely malleable offering exciting possibilities to allow decoration to alter the form. Drawing on the surface of the soft form with a range of tools from potters' needles to hacksaw blades will give large numbers of lines and marks of differing quality. If the forms are thinly made, care must be taken not to tear the clay wall.

Although a very dense material, porcelain clay is often thixotropic, and can become very soft, almost fluid when compressed. This can be exploited when working with the surface of slabs or sheets of clay. Slicing blocks of clay with wires of different thickness and then manipulating these thick slabs by stretching and slamming onto a wooden tabletop can produce surfaces that tell a fresh story about the nature of porcelain.

Janet DeBoos, 'decorating is by the act of throwing'. Pourer, Height: 18 cm (7 in.).

Rojie Koie. Cup with incised lines.
Photograph, Galerie Besson.

Jack Doherty. Carving a soft thrown cup.

Edmund de Waal. Bowls with impressed seals.

Leatherhard clay

More precise marks and drawing can
be achieved when the clay has begun
to dry. A thin scalpel or craft knife
blade can be used to draw and engrave
into leatherhard clay. Drawn marks
can be emphasised by inlaying washes
of oxide or slip, or be allowed to fill with
pooled glaze.

Yuk-kan draws directly onto the
leatherhard clay using a pin or a pencil.
The drawings are developed and given
greater depth by adding oxides and
underglaze colour after biscuit firing.
She writes, 'I like to draw. I work on the

Jack Doherty. Slab dish with wire-cut surface.

Yuk-Kan Yeung. Bottle, (detail).

porcelain form as I work on a piece of paper, only this is three-dimensional paper. It makes my drawing more interesting; as one turns the form around different compositions will appear.'

The smooth, fine grained quality of porcelain clay is especially suited to carving techniques. Sharp blades can be used to cut relief decoration into the surface of leatherhard forms. Some of the most sensitive decorations in the history of ceramics can be found in the carved and celadon glazed pots from Song Dynasty China.

Colouring clay

The whiteness of porcelain can be an invitation to make additions and alterations to the clay body itself, to alter its colour or texture. Commercial body stains are often used. While manufacturers recommend amounts of 10% to 20%, much smaller additions will give good results in a pure porcelain clay.

Ruthanne Tudball. Jar with carved surface, soda-fired.

Subtle colours can be produced by adding as little as 1%. Stains or oxides can be added to small quantities of clay by kneading or wedging. This can be a laborious method and for larger amounts it is more efficient to mix the clay as a thick slip and then reconstitute it.

A reliable way of mixing coloured clays is to begin with a quantity of dry porcelain. I use the turning scraps from the wheel. These are small enough to soak down easily. Porcelain is a very dense material – unlike stoneware or earthenware there is no sand or grog to open the clay. Therefore slaking this clay can be more difficult. Using hot water will help. First weigh the stain or oxide, mix with water then sieve this through a 100s mesh into a quarter bucket of hot water. Stir thoroughly before slowly adding the measured amount of dried clay. Mix to a thick slurry, soak overnight, then dry to a usable consistency

on a plaster bat or in a bisque bowl.

Commercial body stains and colours are formulated and produced for the ceramics industry and will give consistent and reliable results. The even quality of the colour may seem a little bland to some artist potters. It is possible to modify commercial colours by adding small amounts of oxides such as rutile or ilmenite. Experiment with amounts from 1% to 5%. It is also possible to make one's own stains from combinations of oxides; these will give interesting but less predictable colours. I make a number of stains which can be used as painting pigments or to colour slips or clay bodies.

I constantly test clays and colours. New tests are first tried singly on a small disc of white porcelain. The successful ones are then used to produce sample discs experimenting with interesting combinations of colours.

Jack Doherty. Coloured clay samples.

Susan Nemeth. Plate with inlaid clays.

Slip

Slip can be used to change both the colour and texture of the porcelain body. Joanna Howells uses a thick application of a white porcelain slip made from her Limoges clay body which she combs and marks whilst it is still wet, producing a fluid rippling quality which forms a soft skin on her thrown and altered forms.

More abrasive textures can be developed with materials such as silicon carbide, which will give pitted and volcanic surfaces during firing.

57

Joanna Howells. Thrown forms with white slip surface.

Pouring slip on the inside of a large bowl which is still attached to a bat.

Pouring out excess slip holding the bat.

Emmanuel Cooper. Jug form, *Urban 1*, silicon carbide slip and glazes. Height: 23 cm (9 in.).

Emmanuel Cooper paints a silicon carbide slip on his bowls and jugs to produce his textured surfaces.

I apply a coating of slip containing 3% of copper oxide to the inside of many of my smaller forms. The copper in this slip reacts with the soda vapour, migrating through the kiln, touching and marking the outside of the pots with flashes of lustre and colour.

Slip can be applied to porcelain using all the conventional methods. Care should be taken not to apply heavy coatings of slip to clay which has become dry. This can cause cracking and splitting, especially to thin forms. If work is to be slipped all over then it makes sense to first coat the inside of the form and allow this to become leatherhard before slipping the outside. As well as pouring and dipping, slip can be brushed, sponged, sprayed or trailed. The best starting point for decorating slips is to use the clay body itself, modified with colouring agents such as oxide combinations, or body stains. A direct method of making decorating slip is to use the dry trimmings from turning. They can be weighed accurately and will slake down evenly. I first weigh the colouring ingredients, then quarter fill a bucket with hot water, add the colouring material to the water and stir thoroughly, weigh and add the dried porcelain clay slowly, sprinkling it into the water. Using hot water helps to dissolve the clay quickly. If possible, leave the mixture to soak overnight. Stir or mix the crude slip – a power mixer will help speed the process – adding more water if necessary. Sieving the slip through 100s mesh should produce an even speckle free material. Because the clay content of the slip contains no impurities such as iron, and is very white, small amounts of oxide and body

stain, from 0.5%–1% can produce subtle and interesting colours. Try experimenting with oxide combinations and varying the percentage additions to the base slip. It is possible to make homemade body stains which can produce less refined surfaces as a contrast to the purity of commercial colours.

All of the usual slip decorating processes can be used on porcelain clay. For example, inlay, sgraffito, wax and paper resist are all used effectively by porcelain makers. It is worth experimenting with these techniques singly or in combinations.

Engobes

Slips or engobes can be applied to biscuit fired porcelain. This can be a useful process when decorating very thinly made pieces.

Feldspar	60
China clay	40

This is a well known and reliable recipe for use on biscuit ware. Try additions of body stain or oxide.

Painted surfaces

The history of ceramics is rich with examples of painted decoration on porcelain. The source of some of the most outstanding painting is China, where great fluency of brushwork is evident. Chinese potters mastered the craft of painting on clay with monochrome underglaze and vibrant onglaze enamel. In the late 12th century, potters resolved the difficulty of introducing colour into high fired ware by applying lead based coloured glazes to pre-fired work. These pieces were then fired for a second time to between 800°C/1472°F

Prue Venables. Bottle and jug. Height (bottle): 20 cm (8 in.), (jug): 13 cm (5 ⅛ in.).
Photograph by Terence Bogue.

and 900°C/1652°F in a kiln in which they were protected from the flame.

The introduction to China of cobalt as a colouring pigment occurred in the early part of the 14th century. Where copper had been used previously, the mastery of underglaze blue decoration was one of the last great developments of Chinese ceramics.

Pigments and colours

The raw metal oxides which we obtain from potters' suppliers can produce harsh, even crude colours when applied to porcelain. But they can be mixed and combined with other minerals to produce far more subtle results. These colours are prepared by weighing the ingredients, thoroughly mixing them with hot water then sieving through a 100s mesh. Always take care when working with metal oxides – use protective gloves and avoid contact with the skin. This can be a messy process, so to avoid contamination at a later date, it is important to clean equipment very carefully.

Whereas the making of painting pigments would have been a painstaking and time consuming process in early potteries, today there is a wide range of underglaze and enamel colours readily available to modern potters. These materials are refined and give very consistent results. Some makers find the quality of the fired colour can be bland; it is possible to add small amounts of

Pigments which can be used for painting or as body and slip stains

Soft green		Dark sea green	
China clay	40	Chrome oxide	35
Flint	35	Cobalt oxide	10
Feldspar	25	Tin oxide	15
Red iron	8	Flint	15
Chrome oxide	16	Alumina	25
Cobalt carbonate	2		
Copper carbonate	2		

Black		Blue	
Chrome oxide	25	China clay	40
Cobalt oxide	10	Feldspar	20
Alumina	25	Flint	15
Iron oxide	30	Nickle oxide	45
Manganese dioxide	15	Cobalt oxide	45

Chocolate brown		Blue	
Chrome oxide	25	Copper oxide	40
Iron oxide	25	Tin oxide	75
Manganese dioxide	10	Cobalt oxide	2
Alumina	40		

oxides to the commercial product which will alter the colour and surface quality.

A contemporary approach to the painted porcelain surface is apparent in the work of Australian potter Prue Venables. She brushes a mixture of 50% iron oxide and 50% cobalt oxide on to the exterior of her forms. This produces a beautiful dense lustrous surface when glazed and fired in a reduction atmosphere.

Sally MacDonell brushes a solution of copper oxide and water onto her figure forms. This is then washed away, leaving a deposit of copper in the cracks and crevices created in the building process. She then paints on a coating of a white stoneware engobe. The pieces are fired to 1165°C/2129°F in an electric kiln. Her surface patterns are created by wrapping parts of the form in tape and firing the 'parcelled up' figures in a smoke kiln

Sally MacDonell. Seated figure (detail), smoked porcelain. Height: 32 cm (12 ½ in.).

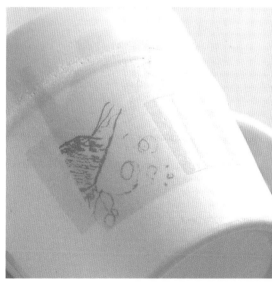

Victoria Bryan. Mug, (detail). Glaze and transfer decoration.

63

Victoria Bryan: 1. Cutting image from the printed enamel sheet.

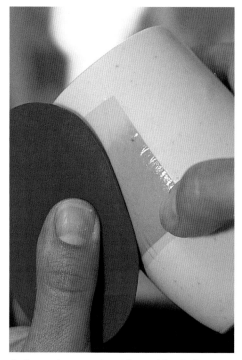

3. Squeezing out air with a rubber kidney.

2. Applying transfer to the pot.

Right 4. Brushing on glaze in masked area.

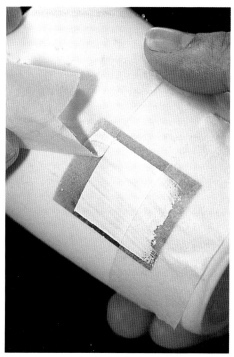

5. Removing mask when glaze is dry.

6. Selecting final image.

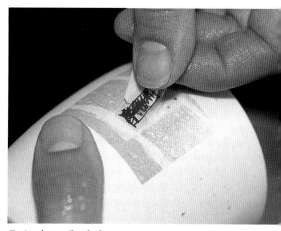

7. Applying final platinum image.

filled with newspaper and sawdust. The fired figures are cleaned with turpentine and finished with several layers of beeswax polish.

In recent years exciting new materials have been added to the potter's repertoire. Underglaze crayons, for instance, enable a way of drawing directly onto the white surface of the clay. Victoria Bryan combines drawing with ceramic pencils and painting with stains to make delicate images on her thrown forms. She controls the glaze application to make a complex surface which has some of the qualities of a watercolour painting.

Applying colour in large areas is a characteristic of some of Peter Lane's work. He uses an air brush to produce subtle, graduated colour changes on his thinly thrown and turned bowls.

Underglaze colours, body stains or oxides can be applied in this way. Colours can be oversprayed but it is important to test these, as ceramic materials can produce unexpected reactions in combination. Spraying and air brushing can be used with resist and masking techniques to build complex decorations.

The whiteness and purity of glazed porcelain has been used as a background for coloured onglaze decoration since the 15th century. Enamel colours which were essentially lead fluxed coloured glazes were used by Chinese

65

potters. The enamel decoration was often combined with underglaze blue painting. The outline of the pattern was first painted onto the clay body, the pot was then glazed and fired in the normal way. The sketched outline of the decoration was then filled with the enamel colour and the work re-fired to temperatures between 850°–900°C/ 1562°–1652°F.

In 17th century Japan, the potters of Arita developed porcelain using the Chinese model of blue underglaze with a coloured enamel. Kamiemon wares in particular were decorated with sensitive combinations of subtle reds, yellows and blues. These pots were frequently copied by European factories. Enamels are essentially low temperature glazes with a firing range of 700°–850°C/ 1292°–1562°F, which fuse to the surface of the fired glaze. Firing enamels can be complicated, as different colours require different firing temperatures and it can be difficult to make enamels adhere to the hard fired porcelain glaze surface.

Russell Coates is a British potter who learned the traditional craft of enamelling in Japan. The recipes which he uses to make his colours are based on traditional materials, some of which are classified as hazardous and should be used with care.

Below Caroline Whyman. Oval forms with gold, platinum, bronze and copper lustre.

Above Chinese garden seat 1850-1920. Porcelain with polychrome enamel painting.
Photograph courtesy of Cheltenham Art Gallery & Museum, UK/Bridgeman Art Library.

Russell Coates. Plate, underglaze blue
and enamels. Diameter: 37 cm (14 ½ in.).

Enamel colours firing range 750°C–850°C/1382°–1562°F
Please note that all lead compounds are hazardous and should be handled with care.

Green		Yellow	
Lead bisilicate	15	Lead carbonate	50
White lead	60	Quartz	20
Quartz	55	Red iron oxide	3
Copper oxide	3		

Purple		Red	
Lead carbonate	50	Lead bisilicate	76
Flint	50	Quartz	4.8
Quartz	10	Borax Frit	46
Manganese oxide	10	Red iron oxide	30

Yellow		Blue	
Lead bisilicate	49.2	Lead bisilicate	78.5
Quartz	4.8	Quartz	1.5
Borax frit	46	Borax frit	20
Red iron oxide	4	Cobalt oxide	0.8

Peter Lane. Airbrushed bowl, 'Mountain sky, evening'. Diameter: 28 cm (11 in.).

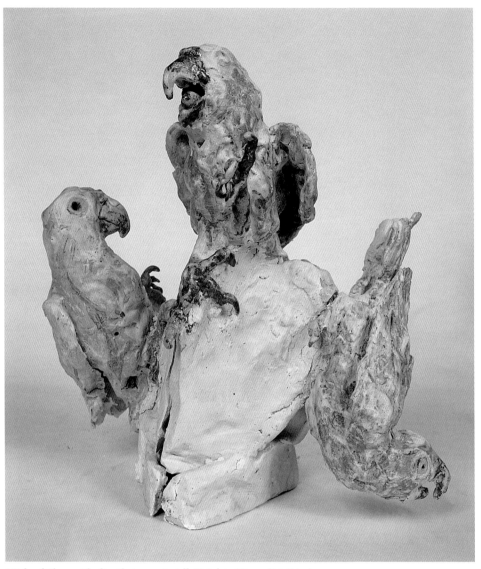

Michael Flynn. *The lies that parrots tell.* Height: 42 cm (16 ½ in.).

Chapter Seven
Firing Processes

Porcelain clay will react with fire more than any other clay. In a negative sense it is liable to slump, warp and distort, with a tendency to develop cracking and firing defects, which can seem endless. It has a memory. Forms which have been altered abruptly or without care will re-tell their story during firing. But when forming and firing is orchestrated by a maker who understands the essential nature of the material, and who is sensitive to the processes involved, then the results can have special, almost mystical qualities. Margaret O'Rorke writes, 'I choose to throw and join thin forms which will reform gracefully during the firing. Encouraging and accepting this is part of my understanding of the nature of the material.' Fire can transform porcelain clay almost to glass. When porcelain is fired to maturity and all the chemical and physical changes which can occur have occurred, then the forms can show a completeness and integration of surface and form which is breathtaking. But it can also mercilessly reveal lack of care in the making.

Biscuit firing

Most potters choose to biscuit fire their work. This first firing makes the ware more durable for safer handling when decorating and glazing. It also renders the clay porous, making it easier to apply a glaze coating. Firing should be seen as a vital and creative part of making, demanding attention to detail at all stages of kiln packing and firing. Packing a biscuit kiln with porcelain is fairly straightforward but there are some danger areas. Dry porcelain is extremely fragile. Care must be taken during handling, moving and packing. It is possible to introduce hairline cracks in fine pieces by picking them up carelessly. This damage can remain unnoticed until after the glaze firing. Kiln furniture should be clean. Shelves must be flat and free from surface irregularities such as uneven build up of bat wash. The work must be packed so that heavy pieces do not damage lighter, thinner ones. Even at biscuit fire temperatures, porcelain can warp and distort. It is important that the work is not placed directly in the flame path – for instance, overhanging the bag wall in a fuel burning kiln or too close to the elements in a electric kiln. Fine rimmed bowls are particularly vulnerable – they can be stacked inside each other or packed rim to rim. It is best not to stack too high as the weight can cause cracking in the pieces at the bottom of the pile. If stoneware is being biscuit fired in the same kiln it can be used to support more fragile porcelain pieces.

Porcelain clays are usually biscuit fired to 1000°C/1832°F. At this fired temperature the clay is still comparatively soft, and can be engraved or incised with a sharp tool. Even after

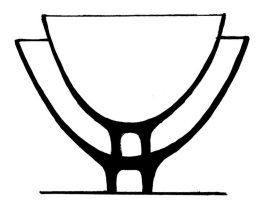

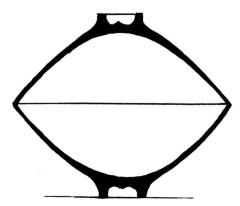

In the biscuit firing work can be stacked. Take care to see that each piece is well supported.

Fine bowls can be packed rim to rim in the biscuit kiln.

biscuit firing it is still more fragile than stoneware or earthenware and care must still be taken when handling complex and thinly made forms. The biscuit fire temperature will affect the porosity of the ware. If this is too high then the work will be more difficult to glaze.

Glaze firing

The nature of porcelain clay demands particular care during the packing of glaze kilns. When fired to its maturing temperature unglazed porcelain has a glassy surface which will cause the work to stick to the kiln shelf. This causes a fault called plucking when small fragments of the base or footring break away, destroying otherwise perfect work. Kiln shelves must be covered with a coating of bat wash. This can be purchased from potter's suppliers, but many potters prefer to mix their own. A mixture of 3 parts of alumina hydrate to 1 part of china clay is adequate for most firings. Bat wash should be used thinly and applied as evenly as possible. If it is allowed to build up on the shelves then the uneven surface can cause warping

and distortion. With certain types of work, large pieces or particularly fine forms, placing them directly on to a thin layer of dry alumina hydrate which has been dusted on to the shelf through a sieve will prevent plucking and allow the work to move and shrink freely during cooling. When using dry alumina, care must be taken to ensure that it does not fall on to other pieces in the kiln. Discs made from the same body as the pots can be biscuit fired, bat washed and used on worn shelves. A wadding mixture of 3 parts alumina hydrate, 1 part china clay and ½ part flour can be mixed with water to a dough-like consistency, rolled into thin sheets, cut to size and used either dry or biscuit fired. It will come away cleanly from the work and does not need to be bat washed. As with biscuit firing the work should be placed so that it is not heated unevenly. Wide forms such as plates or dishes should be positioned so that the entire base or foot is supported. They must not be allowed to overhang the edge of shelves.

Lidded forms can present some problems. Because of the risk of warping, lids should be fired on the pot. As the porcelain clay will become vitrified and glassy, a thin layer of alumina mixed with water carefully painted on to the rim of the pot or lid will prevent the surfaces from welding together. Thin coils of wadding material will also prevent lids from sticking. Susan Nemeth, who makes unglazed porcelain, fires her work buried in saggars which have been carefully packed with silica sand. This helps to prevent warping, particularly in her plates.

Single firing

Porcelain can be successfully once fired; if the work is handled carefully then biscuit firing can be eliminated. Glazing can be done when the clay is dry, using a process adapted to suit particular forms (see Chapter Eight). The main difficulty is to hold and manipulate fragile forms, but with some thought systems can be developed which reduce the risk of breakage. The forms can be designed for raw glazing with features such as strong foot rings to allow the pieces to be handled more easily.

The work should be completely dry before firing. The early part of the firing schedule for once-fired work is similar to that for biscuit, with a slow start, gently firing to around 300°C/572°F, then steadily increasing the temperature rise. The size and type of work being fired will determine just how slow this part of the firing should be. Problems can occur with large forms and pieces with a complicated shape or uneven thickness. Small, thinly thrown work can be fired more rapidly without difficulty.

Oxidised firing

Porcelain clay which is fired in an oxidising atmosphere will have a warmer, creamier colour than that fired in

reduction. This is due to the minute amounts of iron present in the constituents of the clay body. It is a characteristic of the process and should not necessarily be seen as a fault.

An outstanding example of clay and glaze integration is evident in the work of Lucie Rie. She developed an unrivalled sense of surface quality and knowledge of a limited range of materials. Her palette of brilliant colour was developed in the neutral atmosphere of her electric kiln and for many potters her work revealed potential in a firing process which at that time was felt to be in some way inferior to that of a flame kiln.

Electric kilns are available to many potters and students. Modern kilns are efficient, with a high standard of insulation, and are capable of achieving firing temperatures of 1250°C–1300°C/2282–2372°F. They are easily controllable and safe to use, giving the opportunity to use and exploit some of the subtlety of porcelain materials. While the classic effects of reduced iron glazes are not easily obtainable, the clean atmosphere produced by electricity is suited to developing the best from body stains, underglaze colour and enamels. Exciting work is being produced by makers who are experimenting with multiple firings in electric kilns, using the kiln as a tool, a controllable process to build complex and interesting surfaces. Caroline Whyman writes, 'I'm an urban potter so it is difficult to accommodate a gas or wood kiln.' She fires her electric kiln to cone 8 at a temperature rise of 100°C (212°F)/hour with a short five minute soak at the top temperature.

Reduction firing can be achieved in electric kilns, with gas torches used to alter the atmosphere, and in Japan many potters use electric firing to

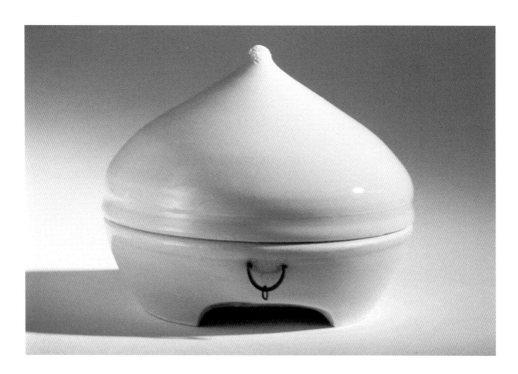

Sandy Simon. Covered jar with nichrome wire, (electric kiln, oxidised). Height: 10 cm (4 in.).

produce celadon glazes. There has been much discussion about the detrimental effect which a reduction atmosphere will have on electric kiln elements. It is wise to discuss this with the kiln supplier before attempting any unorthodox firing procedures. From a health and safety viewpoint always use extreme caution when introducing any combustible material into an electric kiln. Localised reduction effects can be achieved by adding silicon carbide into slips or glazes.

Reduction firing

Many of the great historical examples of porcelain making were the product of fuel burning kilns where the kiln atmosphere was essentially reducing, or alternating between reduction and oxidation. Reduction firing makes possible a wide range of colour and surface from a relatively small number of materials. I would suggest that most contemporary porcelain potters who use reduction firings do so in gas kilns, with propane being the most readily available fuel. Essentially the term reduction means removing oxygen from the metal oxides present in clay, glaze and decorating materials. Potters achieve reduction by manipulating the kiln atmosphere during periods of the firing. Reduction can also be used during cooling to obtain particular effects from glazes and lustres. A reduction atmosphere results from an excess of carbon in the kiln atmosphere. When the kiln atmosphere is overloaded with carbon, the materials being fired cannot obtain enough oxygen to ensure complete combustion. Carbon monoxide gas is formed which, in order to become carbon dioxide, removes oxygen from the metal oxides in the clay and glaze materials. Reduction causes dramatic colour changes in some oxides. Particularly important to porcelain makers are the reduced qualities of iron and copper oxide in slips and glazes. In oxidation, iron oxide will produce a range of yellow to brown colours. In reduction firing it will give the celadon colours which vary from the palest blue to dark green. Used in amounts of 8% to 10% it can produce rich blacks. Copper oxide fired in an oxidising kiln will give green to turquoise while in reduction it can give blushes of pink through to rich reds.

Reduction firing will also alter the colour of the unglazed clay body by affecting the small amounts of iron present, changing the clay from the cream colour and warm tone associated with oxidised firing to the characteristic cold whiteness of reduction. It is difficult to give precise instructions on how to achieve good results in reduction firing,

as so much depends on the kiln, its fuel and burner system, the type of work and the slips and glazes being used. However there are guidelines and advice from experienced potters which may help.

The most straightforward schedule is to fire in oxidation to 1000°C/1832°F (cone 06), then to introduce a light reduction (by altering burner settings or adjusting the damper or both), thereafter maintaining a steady temperature rise until the end of the firing. David Leach fires his small propane kiln to cone 10–11 in 7 ½ hours, reducing from 1000°C/1832°F until the end. A heavy reduction atmosphere is usually unnecessary and can slow the firing considerably. It can sometimes be useful to alternate periods of reduction and oxidation.

Victoria Bryan. Two bowls, fired in an electric kiln. *Photograph by Howie.*

I fire to cone 06 trying to keep a temperature climb of 100°C/212°F an hour. I then begin a light reduction by pushing in the slide damper until a gentle flame is visible at the centre spyhole. It is possible also to detect reduction conditions by a characteristic smell. Combustion atmospheres can be measured accurately by using an oxygen probe. I have four 20-minute periods of heavy reduction at intervals of 50°C/122°F. That is, 1050°C/1922°F, 1100°C/2012°F, 1200°C/2192°F and 1250°C/2282°F. When cone 10 is flat, I soak for 15 minutes then switch off, clam up the kiln and cool slowly.

Margaret O'Rorke begins a heavy reduction at 960°C/1760°F holding the temperature steady for one hour, she then continues the firing with a light reduction to 1250°C/2282°F with a

period of oxidation up to 1300°C/2372°F before ending with a soak of two hours. This cycle gives her work a surface which transmits light, and also intensifies the translucency and clarity of the body.

Wood firing

Firing the purest, whitest porcelain clay in a wood kiln which is subject to temperature variations and deposits of fly ash could be thought an eccentric occupation. But when the making and firing processes are understood and used sensitively, wood firing can add a unique quality to porcelain forms. Gwyn Hanssen Pigott lives and works in Queensland, Australia. She makes some of the most subtle and moving contemporary porcelain using a wood fired kiln.

She chooses to fire her Limoges porcelain pieces in the parts of her kiln which attract only the finest deposit of

Gwyn Hanssen Pigott. Oval bowl, wood fired. *Photograph by Brian Hand.*

ash. The effect of the ash is quiet, barely noticed, but it adds a vital change of tone or cloudiness, softening the form and showing the mark of the flame path. As with all methods of firing porcelain, wood firing demands meticulous care and attention to detail. Wood firing presents the added hazard of fly ash which is drawn through the kiln and deposited on the pots. It can cause the work to stick to the kiln shelf. Gwyn Hanssen Pigott fires her work on flat pads of wadding material. A common mix is 3 parts alumina to 1 part refractory ball clay. Choosing a clay which is low in iron will reduce the risk of contamination on the base of the work. These pads are dried carefully to keep them flat and then biscuit fired. They can be reused, with any ashed areas painted over with bat wash. The positioning of work in a wood kiln involves both practical and aesthetic issues. Gwyn uses a long firing cycle of

about 26 hours. Porcelain clay will soften significantly as it approaches maturation. She finds that the Limoges porcelain can soften too much and collapse if not protected from the fiercest flames. Experience of firing and knowledge of the kiln play an important part in achieving consistent results.

If firing porcelain in a wood kiln for 26 hours is considered eccentric, then firing it in an anagama kiln for five days must seem idiosyncratic in the extreme. The long firing cycle, high temperatures, and atmosphere variations of the anagama process do not seem immediately compatible with conventional ideas about porcelain.

However, there are a few potters prepared to gamble with fire. Jack Troy lives and works in Pennsylvania. While the majority of the production from his anagama is stoneware he regularly fires

Jack Troy. Porcelain cups, Anagama fired.

grolleg based porcelain clays. His cups and vases are usually shino glazed with a colour range from pink to orange, often showing dramatic black surface markings from carbon trapping. The anagama firing cycle induces intense heat and encourages the distribution of large amounts of ash. Porcelain is perhaps best fired in saggars or protected from the direct flame by pots made from more refractory clays.

Jack fires his kiln for five days, soaking at the top temperature for around 30 hours. The long soak does much to develop the extraordinary depth and subtlety in the shino glazes. The kiln is allowed to cool slowly in a reduction atmosphere for some of the time. This helps to develop the characteristic orange and red colours derived from the minute quantities of iron present in the kaolins.

Vapour glaze

Many potters use sodium vapour glaze very successfully with porcelain. Whether in the form of sodium chloride or sodium carbonate or bicarbonate this process offers a wide range of surface and colour qualities. At its best it can accentuate the surface quality of porcelain clay without concealing its delicacy. Salt or soda glazing depends on the reaction between sodium, which is a flux, and silica, which is the main glass former in clays, slips and glazes. Alumina, which does not react with sodium will also affect the quality of the glaze, as will the iron content of the materials, which can have a dulling effect on the glaze. Porcelain clays high in silica will react easily with salt or soda, producing a shiny, finely crazed glaze surface. The make up of porcelain

Jack Doherty. Eight cups, vapour glazed. *Photograph by Sue Packer.*

clays with their high kaolin and low iron content gives potters the option to explore a range of surface qualities, from the gentle pink or orange colours of a minimal sodium glaze, to the familiar rich 'orange peel' texture of salt glaze. Often simple combinations of ball clays and kaolins will produce the most satisfying results, showing the trace of the fire.

I find that delicately flashed surfaces can be produced on porcelain with thin applications of slip, fired in a reduction kiln with light salt or soda. For these colours I spray 1.5 kg (3 lb 5 oz) of sodium bicarbonate mixed with 6 l (10.5 UK pints or 12.5 US pints) of hot water into a 20 cu ft kiln. Reduction

Ruthanne Tudball. Teapot, soda glazed.

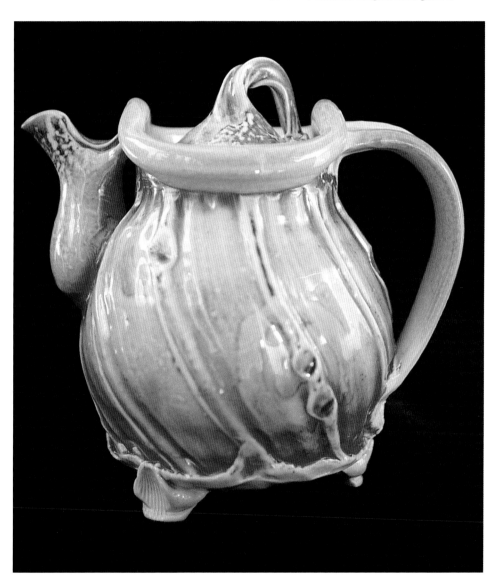

Slips for salt or soda firing

Pale pink	orange	yellow	apricot
66 porcelain clay	33 porcelain clay	90 porcelain clay	80 porcelain clay
33 china clay	33 china clay	10 titanium dioxide	20 titanium dioxide
—	33 AT ball clay	—	—

AT ball clay has an analysis of: SiO_2 52
Al_2O_3 30
Fe_2O_3 2.6

Ruthanne Tudball's slips

Black slip		orange slip	
AT ball clay	33	Ball clay (1.5% iron)	50
Porcelain clay powder	33	Grolleg china clay	50
Soda feldspar	33		
Black stain	15		

Back stain	
Chrome oxide	54
Red iron	26
Manganese dioxide	44
Cobalt oxide	5

begins at Orton cone 06 until the end of the firing when cone 10 is flat. Spraying begins just as cone 8 is beginning to soften and takes approximately an hour and a half. When all of the soda mixture has been sprayed, the firing continues until cone 10 is flat, then ends with a soak of 15 minutes.

Different ball clays and kaolins will give subtley different results and it can be worth experimenting, bearing in mind the relationship of silica to alumina. Suppliers are happy to provide data sheets for their clays.

Ruthanne Tudball throws and facets soft Limoges clay. Her fluid forms and rich surfaces are beautifully accentuated by the directional quality of soda vapour glaze. Her slips are applied fairly thickly and are often covered with a wash of rutile.

Chapter Eight
Glaze

In Song dynasty China, the pots which we regard as some of the finest examples of porcelain would have been glazed with mixtures of natural materials which were often technically impure, but which produced glaze surfaces and colours of unrivalled visual quality. In the West, the search for a porcelain technology has always focused on refinement, seeking to achieve the quality of Chinese wares through using the purest available materials. While the ceramics industry has evolved production glazing and firing methods of great sophistication, it has perhaps been at the expense of the subtlety and interest displayed in these early Chinese pots.

In recent years, clay suppliers have produced porcelain bodies to suit a large number of firing techniques and temperatures. It is now possible to buy clays which fire between 1220°C/2192°F and 1400°C/2552°F. This has given studio porcelain makers scope to experiment with a wide range of firings and to develop and extend the range of glaze colour and surface.

In lower fired ceramics such as earthenware there is a distinct difference between the glaze layer and the clay. Essentially the glaze is a coating of glass which is fused to the fired clay body with little interaction between them. With high fired ceramics, particularly porcelain, a body glaze interface develops which is often thicker than the remaining layer of pure glass. This intermediate

Margaret O'Rorke. Horizontal hanging pods. Height: 16 cm (6 ¼ in.). *Photograph by Richard Heeps.*

layer has both aesthetic and functional implications. Well-fired glazed porcelain is certainly stronger than unglazed – the interface can cushion and absorb stress between clay and glaze. The fusion of glaze and body can also give great depth to transparent and semi-opaque glazes such as celadon.

When fired to maturity porcelain clay is densely vitrified and is in a sense more akin to glass than bisque. One of the most minimal surface enhancement techniques is used by Margaret O'Rorke.

She brushes a thin solution of feldspar and water directly on to her thrown forms whilst they are still wet. This gives her work a surface from which the light is deflected as well as transmitted without obliterating the definition of the making process.

Enhancing the clarity of colour and translucency of the porcelain clay is a task which has been tackled by potters over many centuries. With high firing temperatures, interesting glazed surfaces can be produced using a small number of very common materials.

Caroline Whyman. 'Illusion vases' inlaid blue porcelain. Height: 16–21 cm (6 ¼–8 ¼ in.).

Simple glazes – 1250°C/2282°F

Try experimenting with mixtures of the clay body you are using and a flux.

Porcelain clay 60
Feldspar 40

Porcelain clay 60
Petalite 40

Porcelain clay 60
Wollastonite 40

Porcelain clay 60
Nepheline syenite 40

Electric kiln glazes

The raw heat of an electric kiln is in some ways extremely appropriate for firing porcelain. It provides a clean and controllable firing, with fairly predictable results. The art of achieving exciting results with an electric kiln lies more in the skilful formulation of slips and glazes than in the firing effects. Lucie Rie was perhaps the greatest exponent of electric firing, producing colours which have a jewel-like brilliance. Many contemporary makers, too, use electric firings with great success, and have developed a new language of colour and texture. The surfaces which they produce range from the delicate satin matt finish on Victoria Bryan's cups and bowls, to the pitted, volcanic jug forms made by Emmanuel Cooper.

Please note all listed cones refer to standard Orton cones.

Recipes for electric kilns

Victoria Bryan, cone 6

Soda feldspar	45
Whiting	20
Zinc oxide	10
China clay	20
Flint	5

Pale Green similar to a pale celadon, Cone 6

Cornish stone	50
China clay	5
Flint	25
Dolomite	3
Zinc oxide	2
Whiting	15
Copper carbonate	1.0

Janet DeBoos, cone 8

Potash feldspar	38
Whiting	20
China clay	12
Silica	30
Dolomite	5
Zinc oxide	5
Bentonite	3

Cone 5/6 Matt

Nepheline syenite	50
Barium carbonate	10
Frit	5
Whiting	5
Lithium carbonate	5
China clay	10
Flint	15

Cone 5/6 Transparent

Potash feldspar	35
Gerstley borate	23
Barium carbonate	8
Whiting	8
China clay	8
Flint	18

Cone 8 Satin matt

Potash feldspar	63
Dolomite	18
China clay	19

Cone 8 Opaque

Potash feldspar	38
Whiting	7
Talc	12
Flint	26
Zirconium silicate	8

Cone 6 Transparent

Flint	18
Soda feldspar	40
Wollastonite	10
Ball clay	12
Gerstley borate	16
Zinc oxide	4

Cone 7 Matt green

Barium carbonate	11
Lithium carbonate	8
Whiting	3
Nepheline syenite	77

Reduction glazes

To some extent most stoneware glaze bases will 'work' when applied to porcelain. Whether or not they will enhance the work is a question of aesthetics. Reliable stoneware glaze bases can be used as starting points to make glazes for porcelain. Adjustments may have to be made to deal with glaze fit problems such as crazing. Base glazes may also need adjusting to suit particular techniques such as underglaze painting or to allow for the thick application necessary for some effects.

If the principal objective is to achieve whiteness, purity and translucency then glazes can be evolved using simple recipes and a small number of basic materials which will give pleasing results, emphasising the cool qualities of reduced porcelain.

Reduction base glazes

Cone 9/10 Satin matt

Talc	23
Potash feldspar	26
China clay	22
Whiting	13
Flint	22

Cone 9/10 matt

Cornish stone	30
China clay	20
Whiting	20
Talc	10

Cone 9 Speckled purple

Cornish stone	40
Feldspar	34
Whiting	9
China clay	17
Copper oxide	2
Rutile	2

Cone 9 transparent

Whiting	32
Flint	35
China clay	33

Cone 9 Crackle glaze (Joanna Howells)

Flint	16.8
Potash feldspar	32
China clay	16
Wood ash	32
Whiting	3.2

Cone 9 Transparent (Gwyn Hanssen Pigott)

Potash feldspar	23
Whiting	14
Talc	6
China clay	22
Flint	35

Flint	20	Whiting	14
China clay	20	China clay	15
Calcium borate frit	10	Calcium borate frit	21
Low expansion frit	50	Low expansion frit	15

Celadons

Of all of the glaze surfaces used on porcelain the range of colours which Western potters and collectors call celadon is one of the most evocative. This family of glazes has a colour range from pale blue to a dark green. The characteristic colours achieved by contemporary potters are the result of using small percentages of iron oxide in a base glaze, fired in a reduction atmosphere. In practice, good results can be achieved by following some straightforward guide lines. Using standard reduction glaze bases for example:

Semi-matt	*Transparent*
Potash feldspar 25	China clay 10
China clay 25	Whiting 20
Flint 25	Flint 30
Whiting 25	Potash feldspar 40

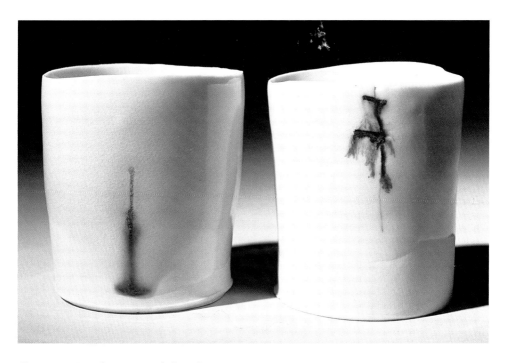

Chun Laio. Porcelain cups, celadon glaze.

Celadon recipes

<table>
<tr><td colspan="2">Cone 8</td><td colspan="2">Cone 8</td></tr>
<tr><td>Potash feldspar</td><td>42</td><td>Potash feldspar</td><td>50</td></tr>
<tr><td>Flint</td><td>27</td><td>Dolomite</td><td>6</td></tr>
<tr><td>Whiting</td><td>18</td><td>Ball clay</td><td>12</td></tr>
<tr><td>China clay</td><td>13</td><td>Whiting</td><td>10</td></tr>
<tr><td>Yellow ochre</td><td>3</td><td>Zinc oxide</td><td>2</td></tr>
<tr><td></td><td></td><td>Flint</td><td>20</td></tr>
<tr><td></td><td></td><td>Red iron oxide</td><td>1.5</td></tr>
<tr><td colspan="2">Cone 8</td><td colspan="2">Cone 8</td></tr>
<tr><td>Flint</td><td>21</td><td>Nepheline syenite</td><td>42</td></tr>
<tr><td>China clay</td><td>27</td><td>Whiting</td><td>19</td></tr>
<tr><td>Potash feldspar</td><td>19</td><td>China clay</td><td>15</td></tr>
<tr><td>Wollastonite</td><td>33</td><td>Flint</td><td>23</td></tr>
<tr><td>Red Iron</td><td>0.5</td><td>Yellow ochre</td><td>1.5</td></tr>
<tr><td colspan="2">Cone 9</td><td colspan="2">Cone 9/10</td></tr>
<tr><td>Cornish stone</td><td>75</td><td>Potash feldspar</td><td>82</td></tr>
<tr><td>Ball clay</td><td>20</td><td>Whiting</td><td>16</td></tr>
<tr><td>Magnesium carbonate</td><td>10</td><td>Flint</td><td>2</td></tr>
<tr><td>Wood ash</td><td>20</td><td>Red iron</td><td>0.8</td></tr>
<tr><td>Flint</td><td>2</td><td></td><td></td></tr>
<tr><td>Red iron</td><td>1.0</td><td></td><td></td></tr>
<tr><td colspan="2">Cone 8/9</td><td colspan="2">Cone 9/10</td></tr>
<tr><td>Cornish stone</td><td>27</td><td>Potash feldspar</td><td>82</td></tr>
<tr><td>Whiting</td><td>27</td><td>Whiting</td><td>6</td></tr>
<tr><td>China clay</td><td>23</td><td>Flint</td><td>13</td></tr>
<tr><td>Flint</td><td>23</td><td>Red iron oxide</td><td>2</td></tr>
<tr><td>Red iron</td><td>0.75</td><td></td><td></td></tr>
<tr><td colspan="2">Cone 9/10</td><td colspan="2"></td></tr>
<tr><td>Whiting</td><td>16</td><td></td><td></td></tr>
<tr><td>Feldspar</td><td>32</td><td></td><td></td></tr>
<tr><td>China clay</td><td>28</td><td></td><td></td></tr>
<tr><td>Flint</td><td>23</td><td></td><td></td></tr>
<tr><td>Local red clay powder</td><td>12</td><td></td><td></td></tr>
</table>

It is possible to see colour changes occur when different amounts of iron are added. Experiment in the range of from 0.5% to 3%. Smaller quantities of iron will give the paler celadons. Also try different sources of iron – synthetic iron, yellow ochre and iron bearing clays – which can produce subtle changes of colour. The choice of glaze ingredients will also have a bearing on the colour of the fired glaze, as will the fineness of the iron oxide used. Most commercial oxides and glaze materials are finely ground and carefully prepared, but additional iron from trace elements such as iron and titanium in clays will have an important effect on the quality of the glaze. The interaction between iron and titanium will cause a colour change towards green. To produce blue celadons of the yingqing (shadow blue) type, it is necessary to choose glaze materials which have a low titanium content or which have a high iron to titanium ratio.

Whilst it is not particularly difficult to compose a celadon type glaze, application and firing will both have a significant effect on the fired result. The sensuous surface and colour quality which is characteristic of the best oriental celadon relies on a very thick glaze layer – up to 2 mm on 12th century Longquan ware. The rich surfaces of Song Dynasty porcelains were meant to imitate the qualities of jade and were probably attained by dipping the forms several times, the colour deepening with each application. This can be difficult to achieve on thin porcelain forms which quickly become saturated with water from the glaze. Dipping is in some ways a more effective method than pouring. Poured glaze often produces an uneven surface with runs and streaks that will spoil the calm contemplative quality of celadon. One of the most common problems is producing an even, matching thickness on the inside and outside of forms. It may be necessary to devise or combine techniques which allow layers of glaze to be built up, drying the work carefully between each application.

Crazing is a common characteristic of celadon glazes on porcelain, a fine network of cracks in the glaze occurring if the glaze has a lower thermal expansion than the clay body. Porcelain clays are designed for a degree of translucency where most of the silica is in a fused or part fused state; this also produces a body with a low thermal expansion. To make glazes fit, one can adjust the amounts of silica to increase the expansion of the clay, reduce the expansion of the glaze, or make adjustments to both. Replacing part of the china clay content of the glaze with 200s mesh Molochite can help to reduce crazing. Other low expansion materials include zinc oxide, and boric oxide which can be introduced in the form of a calcium borate frit.

The control of the reduction firing is an important factor in producing consistent results with celadon glazes. Iron is extremely sensitive to variations in the kiln atmosphere and can give yellow to green colours when oxidised. There are many individual theories as to how celadon glazes should be fired. The consensus seems to be that a slow firing and cooling cycle with a strong reduction, beginning at cone 01 until the end of the firing can help develop richness and depth of colour in the glaze.

Copper in porcelain glazes

Copper is one of the most effective and versatile colouring oxides available to porcelain makers. The colour response will range from the palest and most delicate blush of pink to the classic vivid copper red. It is also a notoriously fickle material which can sometimes give unexpected colours and effects difficult to reproduce. It will give the widest range of colour in reduction firing, but interesting colours are also possible in electric kilns.

It is probable that the first Chinese copper red glazes appeared during the Tang dynasty (AD618–906) originating possibly as a result of badly fired green copper glazes. The Imperial wares of the Ming dynasty (AD1368–1644) represent the peak of achievement for this type of ware. Rigorous quality control was exercised in the production of these pots which were used in Imperial rituals. Losses were high, with only a small proportion of the fired work deemed acceptable. Whilst high temperature copper glazes are unpredictable and difficult to control, modern potters in Jingdezhen expect a 10% success rate! They are challenging to formulate and to fire.

Copper is sensitive to changes in the kiln atmosphere and reduces easily, the equation being $2CuO+CO \longrightarrow Cu_2O +CO_2$. It will also volatilise readily, leaving colourless areas in the glaze. Very small percentages of copper carbonate from 0.5% to 1.0% can produce good copper reds. An addition of 0.5% iron oxide or 1% tin oxide will help to make the colour more reliable. As with celadons, the thickness of the glaze is critical, and there is evidence that some Chinese copper reds had several layers of glaze applied. Potters also use glazes containing copper as an overglaze, applying it on top of a base coating.

Joanna Howells. Bowl, copper red glaze.

Jack Doherty. Jar, soda vapour glaze. The colour comes from a copper slip applied to the inside of the form. *Photograph by Sue Packer.*

High temperature copper reds

Cone 9/10

Potash feldspar	52
Flint	25
Whiting	9
Colemanite	6
Dolomite	2
Zinc oxide	2
Tin oxide	1
Red iron oxide	1
Copper carbonate	1

Cone 9/10

Nepheline syenite	12
Potash feldspar	22
Flint	33
Colemanite	16
Zinc oxide	9
Barium carbonate	7
Tin oxide	2
Copper carbonate	2

Cone 6

Potash feldspar	60
Frit	11
Zinc oxide	5
Talc	4
Whiting	16
China clay	3
Tin oxide	2
Copper carbonate	1

Cone 6

Cornish stone	87
Whiting	10
Copper carbonate	0.8
Red iron oxide	0.5

Cone 10

Potash feldspar	19
Soda Ash	12
Wollastonite	11
China clay	32
Calcium borate frit	12
Flint	10
Tin oxide	1.0
Copper carbonate	0.3

Cone 8

Potash feldspar	54
Flint	22
Whiting	12
Red iron oxide	0.5
Copper carbonate	0.8

Metallic surfaces

Heavy concentrations of oxide can produce interesting decorative surfaces on non-functional porcelain forms. Combinations of manganese copper and iron can give metallic surfaces with colours close to gold and bronze. They emphasise the precious quality of porcelain and can be used on their own, or combined with a coloured glaze, creating essentially non-functional surfaces. They can be fluid, volatile mixtures which must be used with care, and are easily overfired, causing spectacular destruction to kiln shelves as they flow freely. Work should be placed on a piece of broken shelf, or on a clay or wadding material disc which can be easily removed after firing.

All of the recipes given should be seen as the starting point for experiment. Different kilns and firing cycles play an important part in the way glazes

Metallic glaze recipes

Cone 6		Cone 6	
Copper oxide	25	Feldspar	25
Manganese dioxide	48	China clay	25
Ball clay	12	Copper oxide	25
China clay	15	Manganese dioxide	25

Cone 6		Cone 6	
Manganese dioxide	70	Manganese dioxide	40
Powdered red clay powder	30	Copper oxide	5
Copper oxide	10	Cobalt oxide	5
		Powdered red clay	60
		Flint	5
		Ball clay	5

Lucie Rie. Bowl with metallic manganese glaze. Diameter: 16 cm (6 ¼ in.).

behave. Whilst most glaze materials are consistent, some may vary from country to country. Ball clays and kaolins, in particular, may have different compositions which will affect glazes.

Glaze application in the studio

Developing interesting recipes is only one part of the glazing process. Colour and surface quality will vary according to the glaze thickness, method of application and type of firing. Applying the glaze layer to porcelain forms is in theory fairly straightforward. There are however a few problems specific to the material and type of form, which can be avoided with care and a little planning. Glazing is usually the final creative act in the making process, and is often hated both by students and more experienced potters. A well applied glaze surface will unify a form. But if the work is glazed in a careless way then the variation in colour and surface quality caused by uneven thickness, drips and runs will destroy the completeness of the form.

Many problems arising in the glaze application, and subsequent firing problems, are caused by lack of planning. Glazing should be carried out in an organized uncluttered space. The work should be sorted into groups for each glaze or glaze combination, taking into account the special qualities of each glaze. Transparent glazes over underglaze painting, for example, may need to be applied more thinly than celadons. Check the consistency of the glazes. This can be done by dipping a biscuit fired or raw test piece. It is useful to apply test glazes in a controlled way, so that the effect of differing thickness can be seen.

A rudimentary way of gauging glaze build up is to count 'seconds' while the test tile is immersed in the glaze.

Measuring the pint weight of the glaze will give an indication of the density of the glaze. This is done by weighing the measuring jug, then measuring and weighing one pint of the glaze slop. Subtract the weight of the jug. The measurement is expressed as oz/pt. If following a recipe with a given pint weight, it is important to identify if the measurement has used imperial or US measures. 1 US pint = 0.83 imperial pints, 1 imperial pint = 1.205 US pints. My low expansion glaze is one which is used thinly and has a pint weight of 24 oz/pt. A celadon glaze will be used more thickly with a typical pint weight of 28 oz/pt. A glaze hydrometer can be used to measure the specific gravity of the glaze, giving accurate information for mixing repeat batches.

Make sure that the work is clean, dry and free from dust. Thin porcelain forms can be difficult to glaze. If dipped for too long, or if the inside and outside are glazed at the same time, then the work will quickly become saturated. In this case the thin biscuit ware will be unable to absorb any more water from the glaze. The glaze will then start to run, causing uneven streaks that are impossible to repair. Glaze the insides first, tidy any splashes or drips, then dry the work thoroughly before applying glaze to the outside. It can be difficult to achieve an equal thickness of glaze on the interior and exterior of fine forms. With some glazes this may not be noticed but in others the colour development is dependant on thickness. It is always worth taking extra time, even developing unorthodox processes to achieve specific effects. If the inside of the piece is first glazed, make sure that the rim is

Raw glazing dry porcelain.

Dry porcelain is extremely fragile and must be handled carefully.

covered, then paint a band of wax around the rim and partly on the inside. When the wax is dry the outside can be glazed by pouring; then use a finger to wipe away excess glaze from the edge. This must be done as quickly as possible, before the glaze begins to dry.

Gwyn Hanssen Pigott has developed a system for glazing her fine thrown forms: 'After pouring all the inside glazes I wait until they are dry, carefully touch up the rims and then paint the inside with hot wax, a 50:50 mixture of paraffin wax and paraffin. (There are commercially available cold waxes which are safer to use.) Then I dip the pieces down into the glaze for the outside, immediately sponging away any glaze which runs over into the inside.'

The rims and edges of porcelain vessel forms are particularly visually important. Careless glazing can destroy the definition of form. This method can be used to avoid clumsy drips or uneven thickness of glaze on edges.

I once fire my work, glazing when the pots are bone dry. I find that, provided the work is handled carefully, glazes can be applied effectively by dipping and pouring. I have devised a system of

Sponging away splashes of glaze.

glazing which minimises the risk of damage to the pots.

As with biscuit ware, it is important to glaze the outsides and insides separately, leaving time for each layer to dry. Glazing dry clay must be done fairly quickly as the glaze will soften the form, weakening joints and in some cases causing the work to collapse. Lucie Rie raw glazed her work, building up rich surfaces by painting on layers of glaze mixed with gum arabic. Raw glazed pieces must be carefully and thoroughly dried before firing.

Spraying can be an efficient way of glazing complex or exceptionally fine forms. It is better to build up the surface by applying several light coats rather than one single heavy coat. Holding the spray gun too close to the work will cause unsightly drips. Sprayed pieces must be handled with great care, as it is easy to damage the dusty glazed surface with finger marks. Spray drift underneath pieces can cause fine foot rings to stick to kiln shelves during firing, so it is essential to make sure that they are carefully cleaned of glaze prior to firing.

Painting glaze is a technique which has become more popular as commercially produced 'brush on' glazes have become available. They were originally designed for hobby potters and sold in small quantities. They can be applied to either biscuit ware or to dry raw clay. Many potters now make their own brush on glazes by adding sodium carboxymethylcellulose which is known as CMC or SCMC. It is possible to buy this material from certain suppliers. Alternatively, some potters merchants are now making and supplying their own CMC and preservative mix. (See the list of suppliers.)

About 4% by weight is a good starting point for experimenting with CMC. The glaze should be mixed as normal and the correct amount of water added. The CMC must then be mixed thoroughly into the glaze. A high-speed mixer will speed up this operation. Alternatively the glaze plus CMC can be allowed to stand for 24 hours. The completed glaze must then be sieved, a 40s mesh is probably the finest which can be used. It may be necessary to repeat the sieving several times. If the glaze is not going to be used immediately, it is important to add a small amount of a proprietary bactericide.

Peter Lane. Bowl decorated with glaze-on-glaze and sgraffito. Diameter: 20 cm (8 in.).

Chapter Nine
Contemporary Approaches

In the past decade there has been a surge of interest in studio produced porcelain. The range and quality of the work made by contemporary porcelain potters has developed far beyond the trivial and ornamental. Their work has been inspired by an individual response to a host of different sources. Porcelain is now a material which is widely endorsed, and can be used to communicate powerful ideas. There has also been an increase in the number of opportunities for ceramicists to show and sell, helping to increase the audience for new work. The popularity of modern studio porcelain can be linked to the greater appreciation of studio ceramics within the wider art and design marketplace. Modern porcelain pieces are now regularly featured in design and style magazines, as well as in specialist ceramics publications. Its quiet colour range matches the pared down minimalist fashion look of the late 20th century.

It is fair to say that for many potters, users and collectors in the West, it is the quality of fineness, purity and refinement which defines porcelain. While these are intrinsic to high temperature porcelain, some ceramicists are challenging those preconceptions and are producing work which breaks from familiar and comfortable images.

The thrown cups and bowls made by Ryoji Koie do challenge our preconceived ideas. His playful and exuberant forms take those of us who are makers beyond the notion that porcelain is a material to be feared. For those whose appreciation of porcelain is based on the formal qualities of Song Dynasty China or the exquisite workmanship of the most

Ryoji Koie. Bowl. *Photograph courtesy of Galerie Besson.*

technically refined European pieces, Koie's pots will certainly surprise. His apparent 'free and easy' way with the clay, and the sensuous and energetic throwing, are part of a different vision. He uses porcelain almost casually, incising and cutting into the soft surfaces, his finger marks tracing the movement of the wheel. Each of the finished pieces has its own precision and unique resolution. His fluency is the result of a process of learning and practice, showing an understanding and relationship with the material which has grown unconsciously over the years.

Some of the most exciting contemporary work forms links and resonates with historic tradition. The work of Michael Flynn refers to the history of European porcelain. 'Its

Above Michael Flynn. *Catching the Cock.*
Height: 44 cm (17 ¼ in.).
Left Michael Flynn. *Harlequin Dreams.*
Height: 53 cm (21 in.).

associations with concepts of beauty, of
wealth, of power, the themes of the early
figurines also provide both tension and
resonance in terms of the relation
between subject matter and material.'
Flynn has for many years worked with
other ceramic materials and processes.
His raku pieces are well known. After an
invitation to participate in an exhibition
in Germany he became interested in
porcelain. The formal and aesthetic
qualities of the material gave his images
a brightness and a clarity which refresh-
ed longer standing themes in his repertoire and provided new directions both
formally and intellectually. He often
works with major porcelain manufacturers, using their clays and firing
processes to produce small series of
individual pieces. His modelled figures,
energized and dynamic, filled with sym-
bolic possibilities, bond with the early
Meissen pieces of Kaendler. But while
early 18th-century European porcelain

Below Julian Stair. Three jugs.

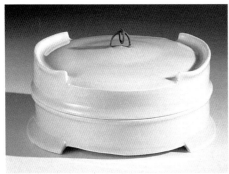

Top Julian Stair. Group of functional
porcelain objects.
Above Sandy Simon. Covered jar with
nichrome wire. Height: 9 cm (3 ½ in.).
Right Edmund de Waal. Jar.

belongs in a world of baroque splendour,
Flynn deals with today's issues and ideas,
his work revitalizing the sometimes
jaded tradition of the porcelain figure.

Function and utility are concepts not
always immediately associated with a
material used to make exquisite objects
which were once valued more than gold.
However, outside of the world of studio
ceramics, the functional properties of
porcelain have long been used in

industry. Electrical conductors, hotel-
ware, sparkplugs, and chemical storage
containers are among the many utilitarian items made from porcelain. But
some contemporary potters are con-
cerned with everyday use, making
practical and beautiful tableware.

Julian Stair writes, 'I throw intentionally thick but well-balanced pots to negate the cliches of porcelain use i.e. translucency and eggshell thinness. My large dinner plates are virtually unbreakable; porcelain can be a very practical clay. I've had tableware going through a dishwasher for over ten years.' He often colours areas of his pots, escaping from the whiteness of the clay.

To American potter Sandy Simon there is a deep connection between the whiteness of the porcelain and its use with food: 'The whiteness is a kind of anticipation, it seems to lie in wait. The wait is for activity with food. In my case this is very important in my motivation for work. I use food in communicating, it [food] – with pots – is a fellowship, almost ritual and certainly sacred.'

Ideas about function, domesticity and ceremony are among those which drive the work of Edmund de Waal. His celadon glazed jars, bowls and beakers with their references to the East, inhabit a special domain. Thrown from soft clay then dented and marked, they are in a sense made to be handled, their forms and surface markings explored in use. They function also as objects of contemplation, things to be cared for.

Janet DeBoos values the fineness and translucence of porcelain and its

Janet DeBoos. *Stoli Bento,* porcelain shot glasses and disposable box. Height (glasses): 6 cm (2 ⅜ in.).

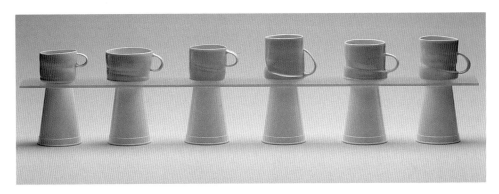

Janet DeBoos. *Reflections On Use*. Porcelain, glass, polystyrene. Length: 60 cm (23 ½ in.).

association with the 'special' rather than the 'ordinary', when it is used in making domestic ware. She is one of a number of artists who have become interested in using vessel forms as part of a group arrangement. Contradicting the conventional idea of a 'matching set', her work includes groupings of forms, which are put together to celebrate the experience of using. She intelligently combines what she describes as 'junk' (polystyrene packaging, etc.) as part of her functional groups. Her groups of domestic pots can be composed of forms which are made and named for specific uses. 'Stolis' are shot glasses (named after a Russian Vodka), 'short blacks' are espresso cups.

Making and living with domestic pottery is at the core of Gwyn Hanssen Pigott's work. Her early workshops in England, France and Australia produced memorable wheel thrown tableware in both stoneware and porcelain. Her recent still-life groupings place common

Gwyn Hanssen Pigott. Still Life group. *Photograph by Brian Hand.*

objects, cups, beakers and bowls in formal arrangements which are rich in subtle relationships of form, colour and surface quality. The individual components are fired in a wood kiln and are gently softened by the touch of the flame and ash. For Gwyn Hanssen Pigott, the firing is not the final creative process. Her groups come into being after she has come to know each of the pieces, sensing their individual qualities, then manipulating and composing with the forms. She is specific about how the work is displayed, insisting on angles of vision which preserve the relationship between the interior and exterior of the pieces.

The potter's wheel is an important element in Daniel Fisher's work too. But his throwing is not a repetitive production process. He makes container forms which are intriguing and difficult to categorise. His pots begin life on the wheel but are then turned upside down and pinched, stretched and manipulated, worked almost to the point of collapse. They can be torn and perforated, the walls of the forms teased to a paper thinness which catches and transmits the light. His gestures and finger markings re-energise the thrown form, giving it a new life. Like Koie, he treats porcelain directly and with a free approach, exploring and enjoying the plasticity of the clay.

Interesting work is produced by ceramicists whose ideas blur the boundaries between function and decoration. Yuk-Kan Yeung was born in Hong Kong and currently lives in Holland. She uses functional forms – dishes, bottles and vases – as vehicles for her decorative

David Fisher. Medium stretched porcelain vessel, 2001. Porcelain, gas fired. Height: 21 cm (8 ¼ in.). *Photograph courtesy of Galerie Besson.*

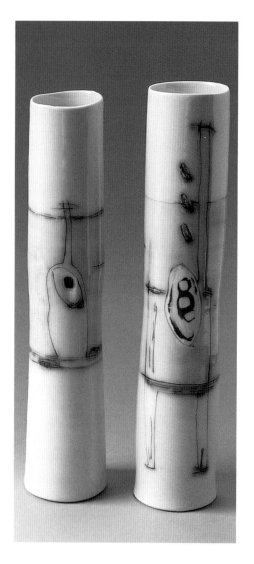

ideas. These come from varied sources: the changing of the seasons, inspiration from music and poetry and everyday objects such as a bottle, chair, table or fruit. She loves to draw, using the porcelain form as 'three-dimensional paper'. Yuk-Kan works intuitively wishing to create a poetic atmosphere which will touch and move viewers.

The way colour is used in contemporary porcelain has evolved in recent years. Traditionally, colour was added by painting under the glaze or applying an enamel decoration on top of the fired glaze. Adding colouring materials such as metal oxide or body stain directly to the clay has now become a popular method of glazing. It allows porcelain potters to decorate their work as part of the making process, integrating surface and form in a way which seems appropriate. Positive but subtle colour is a key element in the work of London-based potter Susan Nemeth. Her work consists of vases, bowls and plates which have a strong decorative element. The decoration is integrated with the form, consisting of layers of coloured clay which have been

Left Yuk-Kan Yeung. Cylinders. Height: 29–30 cm (11 ¼–11 ¾ in.).
Below Yuk-Kan Yeung. Vessel. Length: 33 cm (13 in.).

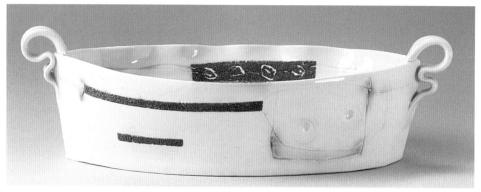

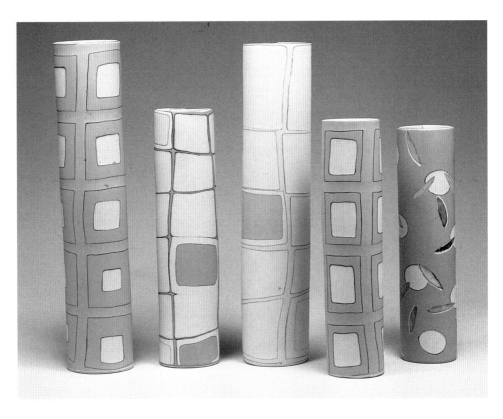

Above Susan Nemeth. Cylinders, inlaid coloured clays.
Right Margaret O'Rorke. *Waves*, light sculpture. Diameter: 42 cm (16 ½ in.).

stained with oxide or body stain. Her surface images are modified and stretched by rolling and press moulding. The stone-like unglazed surfaces are sanded and polished.

The quality of light which is transmitted by the translucency of high-fired porcelain inspires the sculptures and installations of Margaret O'Rorke. All of her work stems from thrown forms, thinly made and often assembled into multiple structures. This exploration of form and translucency has led her to incorporate electric light within her pieces. Her work ranges in scale

Margaret O'Rorke. Light sculpture installation.

from domestic sized lights to large installations for hotels and public spaces. Like Michael Flynn, she has collaborated with industrial manufacturers, producing prototypes for production.

Contemporary makers such as Sally MacDonnell are free to use porcelain clay for its whiteness and purity, firing not for the hardness and translucency of high-temperature porcelain but for the delicate and subtle surface effects obtained when the work is smoke fired. Her handbuilt female figures are constructions made from small sections of porcelain clay and are usually adorned with an imposing headdress. Among her sources of inspiration are ideas from African sculpture. The controlled yet random quality of the smoke marks contrast with the formal posture of the figure and suggests ritualistic markings.

Industrial methods are fundamental to the work of Pieter Stockmans. He is an industrial designer, a maker of artefacts, and an artist who creates large scale installations. Central to all of his work is a love of porcelain which he slipcasts and manipulates with great sensitivity. 'I never insist on making a nice and beautiful form. I wish to express something and it acquires the wanted appearance, as it so happens to grow. I don't go for effects, I just work within the feeling of harmony with the maker. If you use the material in its own natural way, it is difficult to make essential mistakes of form.' He has worked with factories in Holland and Germany designing tableware; his designs range in concept from mass-produced utilitarian hotel and restaurant ware to much freer cast and altered domestic pieces. His way of using and developing industrial techniques has resulted in work which involves the

Sally MacDonell. Standing Figures, smoked porcelain.

factory workers in the creative process. 'As a designer, I have developed a technique in which the workman forms the shape of the vases, and not the designer.' Pieter Stockmans' installations can be seen in many major European museums. This work is linked with his industrial activities. His sculpture frequently uses multiple images, repeated slipcast bowls, and images of faces which have been altered and stretched.

Left Sally MacDonell. Seated Figure. Height: 27 cm (10 ½ in.).

Below Pieter Stockmans. *'Be mindfull o man that thou art but dust, and to porcelain shalt thou return.'*

Bibliography

Birks, Tony, *Lucie Rie*, Alphabooks/A & C Black, 1987

Coatts, Margaret, *Potters in Parallel*, Herbert Press/Barbican Art Gallery, 1997

Cooper, Emmanuel, *A History of World Pottery*, Batsford, 1981

Cooper, Emmanuel, *Ten Thousand Years of Pottery*, British Museum Press, 2000

Freestone, Ian and Gaimster, David, *Pottery in the Making*, British Museum Press, 2000

Gleeson, Janet, *The Arcanum*, Bantam Books,1997

Hamer, Janet & Hamer, Frank, *The Potters Dictionary of Materials and Techniques*, A & C Black, 4th Ed., 1997

Hutchinson Cuff, *Ceramic Technology for Potters and Sculptors*, A & C Black, 1997

Lane, Peter, *Contemporary Porcelain*, A & C Black, 1995

Lane, Peter, *Studio Porcelain*, A & C Black, 1980

Leach, Bernard, *A Potters Book*, Faber & Faber, 1945

Medley, Margaret, *The Chinese Potter*, Phaidon, 1976

Minogue, Coll and Sanderson, Robert *Wood Fired Ceramics*, A & C Black, 2000

Rhodes, *Stoneware and Porcelain*, Chilton/Pitman, 1960

Rhodes, *Clay and Glazes for the Potter*, Pitman, 1969

Sandeman, *Working with Porcelain*, Pitman, 1979

Troy, Jack *Wood Fired Stoneware and Porcelain*, Chilton, 1995

Whyman, Caroline, *Porcelain*, Batsford, 1994

List of Suppliers

United Kingdom

Bath Potters Supplies
2 Dorset Close, Bath, BA2 3RF
Tel: 01225 337046
Fax: 01225 462712
stevemil@btinternet.com
http://www. bathpotters.demon.co. uk

Briar Wheels & Supplies Ltd
Whitsbury Road, Fordingbridge,
Hants, SP6 1NQ
Tel: 01425 652991
http://www.briarwheels.co.uk

Charles Lamb Geotechnics (Lustres)
39 Farleigh Fields, Orton Wistow
Peterborough, PE2 6YB
Tel: 01733 234096

Clayman
Morells Barn, Park Lane
Lagness, Chichester, West Sussex, PO2 6LR
Tel: 01243 2645845
info@clayman.demon.co.uk

Commercial Clay Ltd
Sandbach Road, Cobridge
Stoke-on Trent, ST6 2DR
Tel: 01782 274448
Fax: 01782 206871

Metrosales
Unit 3, 46 Mill Place
Kingston-upon-Thames, Surrey, KT1 2RL
Tel: 0208 546 1078
Suppliers of polyester and nylon fibre

Porcelain Throwing Tools
Jack Doherty
Hooks Cottage, Lea Bailey
Ross on Wye, HR9 5TY
Tel: 01989 750644
jack.doherty@virgin.net

Potclays Ltd
Brickkiln Lane, Etruria,
Stoke-on-Trent, ST4 7BP
Tel: 01782 219816

Potterycrafts Ltd
Campbell Road, Stoke-on-Trent, ST4 4ET
Tel: 01782 745000
Fax: 01782 746000
sales @potterycrafts.co.uk
http://www. potterycrafts.co. uk

Scarva Pottery Supplies
Unit 20
Scarva Road Industrial Estate
Banbridge, Co. Down, BT32 3QD
Tel: 018206 69699
Fax: 018206 69700
david@scarva pottery.demon.uk
http:// www.scarvapottery.com

Valentine Clay Products
The Sliphouse, Birches Head Road
Hanley, Stoke-on-Trent, ST1 6LH
Tel: 01782 271200

W J Doble Pottery Clays
Newdowns Sand & Clay Pits
St. Agnes. Cornwall, TR5 OST
Tel: 01872 552979

USA and Canada

AFTOSA
1034 Ohio Avenue, Richmond,
CA 94804
Tel: 800 2310397
http://www.aftosa.com

Alligator Clay Co.
2721 W. Perdue Ave
Baton Rouge, LA 70814
Tel: 225932 9457
e.s.p.e.s @worldnet.att.net
http:// www.brcentral. com/
southernpottery

American Art Clay Co.
W. 16th Street, Indianapolis, IN 46222
Tel: 317 244 6871
http://www.amaco.com

Axner Pottery Supplies
P.O. Box 621484, Oviedo, FL 32765
Tel: 800 843 7057
axner@ aol.com
http:// www. axner.com

Kickwheel Pottery Supplies
6477 Peach Tree Industrial Blvd.
Atlanta, GA 30360
Tel: 770 986 9011
kickwheel@aol.com

Laguna Clay Co.
1440 Lomitas Avenue,
City of Industry, CA 91746
Tel: 800 452 4862
http://www.lagunaclay.com

Mile Hi Ceramics
77 Lipan Street, Denver, Colorado 80205
Tel: 303 825 4570
http://www.milehighceramics.com

Minnesota Clay Co
8001 Grand Avenue South
Bloomington, MN 55420
Tel: 612 884 9101
http://mm.com/mnclayus/

Tuckers Pottery Supplies Inc
15 West Pearce St., Richmond Hill
Ontario, Canada L4B1 H6
Tel: 800 304 6185
tuckers@passport.ca
http://www.tuckerspottery.com

Australia

Ceramic Supply Co.
17-19 Paves Street, Guildford, NSW 2161
Tel: 612 9892 1566
E mail: csco@bigpond.com

Clayworks Australia
6 Johnstone Court, Dandenong
Victoria 3175
Tel: 613 9791 6749

Northcote Pottery Supplies
854 Clyde Street, Northcote,
Victoria 3071
Tel: 613 9484 4580
E mail: melb@northcote-pots.com.au

Pottery Supplies
S. Castlemain Street, Paddington
Queensland 4064
Tel: 617 3368 2877
E mail: info@potterysupplies.com.au

Walker Ceramics
Boronia Road, Wantirna, Victoria 3125
Tel: 613 9725 7255

New Zealand

Wellington Potters Supplies
2 Cashmere Avenue, Khandallah
Wellington
Tel: 04 939 1211
E mail: twobees@paradise.net.nz

Index